SLIGO

with Cathal Mullaney

www.**HERO**BOOKS.digital

HEROBOOKS

PUBLISHED BY HERO BOOKS
1 WOODVILLE GREEN
LUCAN
CO. DUBLIN
IRELAND

Hero Books is an imprint of Umbrella Publishing
First Published 2021
Copyright © Cathal Mullaney 2021
All rights reserved

A CIP record for this book is available from the British Library

ISBN 9781910827321

Cover design and formatting: jessica@viitaladesign.com
Ebook formatting: www.ebooklaunch.com
Photographs: Sportsfile, Brendan McCauley, Noel Mullaney and Cathal Mullaney

★ DEDICATION ★

To all those who have worn the famous white and black

★ CONTENTS ★

★ ACKNOWLEDGEMENTS ★

WALKING UP WHAT seemed like the highest steps I ever climbed, I finally got a look at the famous sod in the flesh.

Croke Park was being rebuilt at the time – the Hogan Stand was a construction site – but down below, the immaculate green grass looked as magical as it did on television, as I peered down from the Upper Cusack Stand where a number of other locals had also got tickets.

A couple of hours later, we were in dreamland as Sligo produced one of their greatest ever displays to beat Kildare in an All-Ireland qualifier.

The euphoria of that occasion in 2001 was trumped 12 months later when Sligo again returned to GAA Headquarters to stun National League champions Tyrone to progress to the All-Ireland quarter-final. A couple of weeks after, we were back in our seats in the Lower Hogan as they went oh-so-close to beating Armagh, who went on to win the All-Ireland after a replay success over Sligo in Navan a fortnight later. Those days were among the best any of us might ever have as Sligo supporters, but as a young six- and seven-year-old watching on, it seemed like that would always be the way.

Of course, that is never the case, and in sport, irrespective of what code or level, the good times are never infinite. For example, the first Sligo championship game I attended was in the summer of 2000. At the back of the terrace in Markievicz Park in the lashing rain, the half-time score read Galway 0-14 Sligo 0-0.

Being a Sligo follower brings out a whole host of emotions for many – pride, despair, anger, happiness. But above all, regardless of results, success or failure, it's what we are.

To chat through those heady days at the turn of the millennium with the players I and so many others idolised at that time was a real thrill during the course of this project – as it was hearing the inside story to the Connacht success in 2007 and that remarkable summer of 2010 when things went so well but ended so disappointingly.

But this book has helped me get to know some of the pre-2000 stars, of which there are many. And for that I am truly grateful for their time and courtesy in chatting, discussing and remembering their days in black and white.

Of course, this book could include so many more top players our county has had in the last 60 years. This isn't an attempt at drawing up a list of the top 30 – rather, it is an effort at including as broad a range of players as possible to give their summation of some of the great days the county has had in that period.

I am greatly indebted to all of those who agreed to participate. Their willingness to talk, giving generously of their time and insights, is what will hopefully make this book an enjoyable read for Sligo supporters near and far.

We must also remember those who have passed on to their eternal reward in the years since their playing days, and remember their contribution to the county.

I am thankful to Liam Hayes and the team at Hero Books for this opportunity. My thanks too to the Sports Editor of *The Sligo Champion* Emma Gallagher and Austin O'Callaghan of *Ocean FM*. I also owe a debt of gratitude to colleagues in the media for their help in tracking down archive material, in particular from the *Western People*, *Roscommon Herald*, *Tuam Herald* and the Carlow *Nationalist*, as well as Roscommon County Library.

I would particularly like to thank one of the game's outstanding administrators, former Sligo county secretary Tommy Kilcoyne, for his wisdom and advice at the outset of this project, as well as family and friends for their support as always.

It would be remiss of me not to mention my own club Enniscrone/Kilglass, which helped foster my love for our national games and continues to do so. There goes a saying, 'One Life, One Club' – I am proud, and always will be, that mine is Enniscrone/Kilglass.

Finally, let me pay tribute to all of those who have donned the Sligo jersey at any level, in any code, over the course of the association's history. They have given us countless moments of joy, and great memories that will last a lifetime.

Sligeach Abú

Cathal Mullaney
August 2021

NOEL MULLANEY

SLIGO 1-11 ROSCOMMON 3-6
Connacht SFC Semi-Final
Fr O'Hara Park, Charlestown
JULY 10 1962

The heartache of losing to Roscommon in 1962 has never been forgotten by Noel Mullaney, who gave brilliant service to Sligo through the 60s, and also represented Connacht.

★ **SLIGO: N Mullaney**; S Sexton, H McGonigle, M Kilcoyne; P Keane, G O'Connor, P Kilgallon; B McCauley, C Cawley; B McHugh (0-2), B Shannon (0-1), J Killoran (0-2); J Hannon, P Christie (0-1), M Kearins (1-5).

★ **ROSCOMMON:** A Brady; JJ Breslin, J Lynch, O Moran; R Craven, G O'Malley, G O'Brien; B Kyne, G Geraghty; Des Feely (0-1), E Curley (0-1), A White (0-1); Don Feely (1-3), C Mahon (2-0), A Kenny.

THE ACTION

HAVING APPEARED TO have done enough to get across the line – and with most of the crowd thinking the same – Sligo's hopes of progressing to the Connacht final were dashed in cruel fashion when Cyril Mahon's late goal gave Roscommon a scarcely deserved win.

It was Sligo who dominated the vast majority of the exchanges at a packed Charlestown, having overcome the challenge of Mayo after a replay to book their place in the semi-finals.

Despite trailing at half-time by 2-5 to 1-4, and having missed a penalty late in the half, the Yeats County summoned a superb comeback after the break and led by three points heading into the closing stages.

However, Sligo lost the services of Mickey Kearins – scorer of 1-5 in all – through injury in the second period, in what was widely regarded as one of the most physical Connacht Championship matches of the era.

Points from Jimmy Killoran and Brendan McHugh sent Sligo 1-11 to 2-5 in front, and many figured as the final whistle neared that the holders were on their way out.

There was to be one final twist, however, with Des Feely rattling over a point before the game's decisive score arrived.

Cyril Mahon was on hand to crash a final goal to the net for Roscommon and though Sligo had the chance to grab an equaliser, they fell agonisingly short, much to the disbelief of most of the spectators in attendance.

Roscommon went on to beat Galway to win the Connacht title, before losing out to Kerry in the All-Ireland decider.

★★★★★

66

JOHN LEE WAS the Sligo goalkeeper before me.

I played Junior Championship for Sligo for two years and 1959 was my first championship game, when we played Mayo. It was a nice honour to get to play for the county; I always thought it a great pleasure to play for your county and represent your own people.

Even though it was a different time and football has changed a lot to today, we trained through the years and we had a good team, especially in 1965; that was a real good team. Galway struck a winning goal in 1965 in the Connacht final. We always seemed to be unlucky. Even up to more modern times, Sligo have been unlucky.

The year Armagh won their All-Ireland in 2002 is probably the closest Sligo came to winning the big one. The 2002 side was probably ahead of our team in the 60s. To me, looking on, the fitness levels were unreal… the speed of the players, I don't think we were near as fast.

We used to train on the sand dunes in Strandhill.

That was for the Connacht final in 1965. Jim McCabe trained us up to '65, and then a fellow called Jim Ryan, a commandant in the army, came in to train us for '66. I was big and strong at 14-and-a-half stone back then, but for that Connacht final I lost a stone. It was the fittest I ever was in my life.

There was a good bit of running but still, compared to what they do now, it's totally different.

At the same time, we still took it very seriously and I used to be awful tensed up for a game. You wouldn't sleep right the night before! There was a huge interest; people loved their football at that time, but everything about it is so different to now.

One time, I was waiting at the end of the road for a lift when we were playing Mayo in Charlestown. The time went on and on… there was no sign of anyone and, of course, there were no phones at that time. So, it was up to the local publican Jim Flanagan to get me there. There had been some mix up with the car and by the time I arrived they were just ready to go out and play…

That was a lively spin to Charlestown!

When I think back now, I remember some matches from when I was playing, and others I remember nothing about. But, to my mind, the one day I never will forget from my career, until the day I die, is that game against Roscommon in 1962.

It was the saddest year of my football career.

We were happy enough that year after the Mayo match because it was a great win in the first round. The replay was a low scoring affair, 1-7 to 1-6, after we had drawn the first match. I don't have too many memories of that or the drawn game, but the Roscommon game is the one I'll never forget.

We made a few changes ahead of that game. One of them was to move in Jimmy Killoran to left half-forward and put Mickey Kearins into left corner-forward.

I went in one time to a match in Sligo and I was walking across the concrete seats, and there was a match on involving the Sligo minors. I saw this fella jumping for a ball out around midfield and I heard some fella shouting… 'Good man Micheál'.

I asked who was the Micheál?

It was Micheál Kearins. I saw it in him that day. That would have been in 1960. To me, he was one of the best forwards ever in the country. Left or right, he was the greatest ever I saw.

Going in against Roscommon, we were confident, but the thing I always thought about Sligo football was, we were never led to believe that we were better than the opposition. Nowadays every team has psychologists and they're talking and talking to them, but that never was the case with us.

We went up to Charlestown for the match, and it just goes to show how different things were at that time as we didn't tog out in dressing-rooms. Instead, we had to change in a café in Bellaghy, and got lifts in cars to the pitch… and we walked back with the crowd after the match.

When the match started Roscommon went up straight away. Don Feely scored a goal in the first couple of minutes. I can still remember that moment, but one day much later I was in the *Independent* newspaper offices in Sligo and saw a photo of myself in a full-length dive… stretching my hand to the post… the ball just in behind it.

It's a great photo.

They got another goal then from Tony White, a good Roscommon forward. He took a rasper of a shot! I blocked it and the ball went away up in the air… everyone came in running after it.

It was punched into the net.

They had a huge lead on us with two early goals.

I think they scored 2-4 inside of 15 minutes… they only got a goal and two points after that. Once we settled down, Sligo played very well.

We took over after that.

There was a huge crowd in Charlestown that day and I remember well, we were leading. It was awful hard hitting that day – five Sligo players had to go off. The hitting that day… I'll never forget it.

We had used all three of our subs, so Cathal Cawley was hobbling around with a bone broken in his ankle… we couldn't replace him. Padraig Kilgallon got injured that day as well, and I'll always remember a high ball coming in and Padraig came across as a sweeper in behind and sailed into the air to catch it… one of those great catches.

At the end, we got a '50' when we were two points up and into injury time, and from that, Gerry O'Malley got it and went up the field soloing, everyone shouting… 'TIME REF… TIME REF!!!'

If the ball went dead from the kick, it might have been over.

But what happened was… Gerry O'Malley came up the field and sent in a long, high ball. Hugh McGonigle our full-back and a Roscommon fella jumped for it but Cyril Mahon, another forward, stayed down for the breaking ball. I dived for his boot, and I looked behind me then… I saw the ball in the net.

All I could think was… *We're beaten!*

We had Sean Sexton at right full-back, a brilliant player, very determined, but he went on a solo run after that because we had time to equalise. Sean went up the field, passed to Brendan McHugh and the shot went narrowly wide.

A key moment in the game was a facial injury sustained by Mickey Kearins with about 10 minutes to go; he had to leave the pitch and while he was off we missed three frees that he would likely have kicked to see us home. We thought we had the game won.

People in the crowd had left, they were gone down the town thinking we had won it. It has been said it was one of the great tragedies in Sligo football, and it really was.

Afterwards, I cried bitter tears and there were many others doing the same. It was unbelievable.

I don't know even if we did win, would we have beaten Galway... we don't know, and we'll never know. But that year, Roscommon got very lucky. Galway were hammering them in the Connacht final in Castlebar when Aidan Brady jumped up on the crossbar and it broke. And the match was held up for 15 or 20 minutes... Roscommon completely took over when it restarted.

So, they had luck on their side. They also had a lucky win against Cavan in the All-Ireland semi-final – that was the first provincial semi-final that was televised. I was at the All-Ireland final, in the Nally Stand. Kerry got a goal in the first minutes and Roscommon weren't in it at all.

There was only a kick of a ball between Galway and ourselves all through those years.

Another time we went up to Tuam in 1960 when Sligo football was at a low ebb; there weren't many following but we went up anyway and we gave Galway a great game. They had Stockwell and Purcell, 'The Terrible Twins' – Purcell was on the '40' and Stockwell was in at full-forward. Two players made their debuts for Galway that day, John Bosco McDermott and Martin Newell.

I made great friends through football and played with some of the very best. Mickey Kearins was one of the best forwards ever, and another player who was right up there with the best was Nace O'Dowd.

Nace O'Dowd could play anywhere. I played against him in a county final in 1958. That day, he caught a ball about 20 yards out from the goals and he held the ball, fell to his knees, swung the fist while kneeling on the ground and he boxed it over the bar. He was one of the top players in the country.

There was one game in particular, in the Railway Cup in Castlebar against Munster. They tried three different men on him and couldn't contain him. He was brilliant, a great player.

Of course, it's commonplace now that a goalkeeper kicks the ball out but that time, I would have been one of the first goalkeepers who started to kick out the ball. Enda Colleran used to kick it out for Galway but a lot of other goalkeepers then started.

But that time it was different for a goalkeeper; you never passed a ball out, you just kicked it as far as you could.

With the kickout you'd be trying to pick out a man alright. I picked out Kearins one day in Sligo; he caught it just past the halfway line and he turned, took a couple of steps... and over the bar. I'd try and pick a man alright, and might vary it from side to side; it wasn't just down the middle.

One of the sweetest days was when we beat Galway in Castlebar in 1966 to qualify for the Wembley Tournament, a big deal then, and my God, we were delighted. Though we lost to Cavan in Wembley, 3-10 to 1-10, it was a great occasion... video footage of it only surfaced recently. It was great to see it back. That was as good as a Connacht Championship.

The first thing ever I won with Sligo was the GEC competition.

GEC were a big electrical company in Louth. There was a festival on one weekend and we were invited up. We went and hammered Louth, and do you know what we got? We got transistor radios... big long radios and a camera at the end of it. That started me off with photography!

You'd have to regret that we don't have a Connacht medal looking back. It's all about winning, but we did have some successes here and there.

We'd a good club team in Sooey in those years as well; we won one championship in 1959 after we were beaten by Nace O'Dowd and Mullinabreena in 1958. We beat Curry the following year. We lost a couple of other finals as well in the 60s.

I was a sub on the Railway Cup too for a few years and it was nice to get in on that. Aidan Brady was the leading goalkeeper in Ireland at that time; he was from Roscommon and a big man. He got injured in a draw with Munster and the replay was in Croke Park, so I played in that. The Railway Cup had good interest back then and had huge crowds attending.

The late Paudie Sheehy was playing that day, Mick O'Dwyer too. John Dowling was at full-forward, and they beat us.

The 60s and into the 70s were good times for Sligo, but I still have great memories of Sligo in 2002 and being up in Croke Park. The way they moved the ball up the field, kicking scores from a long way out, and beating Tyrone and almost getting over Armagh… it was a brilliant year. Eamonn O'Hara's surging runs and Dessie Sloyan's point-kicking were highlights from that year.

Looking back now, I am glad to have had the honour of representing Sligo and for having made so many great friends along the way.

MICHEÁL KEARINS

SLIGO 2-11 MAYO 2-8
Connacht SFC Semi-Final
Fr O'Hara Park, Charlestown
JULY 4 1965

Mickey Kearins was Sligo's true leader up front, and arguably the greatest forward in the country through the 60s and into the 70s.

★ **SLIGO:** N Mullaney; P Keane, J Killoran, G McManus; M Marren, C Cawley, L Caffrey; B McCauley (0-1), B Shannon (1-0); S Durkin (0-1), M Durcan (0-1), **M Kearins (1-7)**; J Hannon (0-1), J Branley, P Walsh.

★ **MAYO:** J McGuinness; R Prendergast, J Morley, V Nally; E Walsh, J Farragher, E Melvin; C Hanley, PJ Loftus; D Doris (0-1), J Mannion, M Connaughton (0-2); J Langan (1-3), M Ruane (0-1), P Kilbane (1-0). Subs: J Corcoran (0-1) for Mannion, J Gibbons for Hanley.

THE ACTION

ONE OF THE great comebacks in the county's history saw Sligo emerge with a fully merited three-point victory over old rivals Mayo at Charlestown. It also gave them a chance to play All-Ireland champions Galway in the Connacht final.

Mayo, with the benefit of a wind advantage in the first-half, dominated the opening half hour.

Few if any would have given Sligo any hope of emerging as winners when Joe Langan's fortuitous goal shortly after half-time sent Mayo in front, 2-6 to 0-3. It was talisman Mickey Kearins whose second-half goal provided the catalyst for the revival which led to the famous victory.

Sligo, with a youthful line-up, were bolstered by the addition of former Mayo player Bill Shannon, who formed a formidable midfield partnership with Collooney teammate Brendan McCauley.

Up until Pat Kilbane's goal after 22 minutes, Sligo had held their own with early points from Kearins and McCauley, but Mayo took control after Kilbane's major blow. The concession of a soft goal from Mayo's Joe Langan after a long ball into the square, put Sligo in what appeared to be an irretrievable position.

Up stepped Mickey Kearins. The St Patrick's Dromard man kicked two points – one from a sideline ball – and then scored a goal to kickstart the comeback. With renewed confidence, Sligo took a vice-like grip on proceedings and the whole crowd could sense the momentum had changed. Bill Shannon's goal against his native county further confirmed their second-half superiority.

Kearins was on song, and deadly accurate with the opportunities presented – Sligo were level in the 40th minute.

Joe Corcoran, introduced as a substitute, tried to sway the tie back in Mayo's favour with a point, but Sligo were not to be denied. Kearins, Sean Durkin and Mickey Durkin were among the scorers in the closing stages to seal a famous victory.

★★★★★

66

1965 AGAINST MAYO in Charlestown is one of the games with Sligo that stands out most for me.

Sligo never played in Charlestown again afterwards because the Mayo County Board felt it was as much a Sligo venue as a Mayo venue. We had played them before in 1962 in Charlestown as well; it was a draw and we beat them in Sligo in the replay. That was a fairly good team.

We met Roscommon in the next round and were by far the better team but lost, and they went all the way to the All-Ireland final. A bad Kerry team beat them in the final. That was my first championship.

I had played in the league at the end of 1961. The league started after the championship in October. I had played minor in 1960 and '61, and had played senior club football from '57, when I was only 14.

We had a good minor team in 1960, and many of them came into the senior team after that.

That minor team was beaten by Galway in Sligo in the Connacht final by a point and they won the All Ireland. We made a bad move that day – I can't remember who was in charge of the team, but I was centrefield and they brought me to centre-back in the second-half, which was the losing of the game.

We had a very good player at centre-back, Brendan McHugh, who has passed away since… he was a big man. Galway had a good player who had won an All-Ireland with St Jarlath's, Tom Prendergast; he was only small but at half-time they brought me back to mark him and we lost a lot of our scoring power as a result.

I played centrefield for the club, and for the county minors. I liked centrefield; I played there most of my time there for the club apart from the last two or three years, when they were moving me closer to the gate!

When I got into the senior team, I started off at corner-forward.

Paddy Christie was playing full-forward at the time and he used to come from England for games… he had a few brothers playing as well. He was originally from Tourlestrane. He was big and strong… no full-back was getting any ball from him. I got a lot of breaks off him.

That was a fairly good Sligo team. There was no collective training at that time… it would have been 1964 or '65 before we ever got together before a match to train.

I went to school in St Muredach's in Ballina. I was a boarder there, but I never got on the team. I learned most of the game at club level.

As I've said, there were no preparations for games at that time and the game was dirtier than it is now. There were some tough men in those years. When I started playing first nobody knew about me. You'd get some tough attention from backs, and club football was dirty at the time too.

But I came through it pretty much unscathed.

The game was different at that time, but you could move around. In later years I found players stuck more to their positions but in my earlier days I was roaming all over the field. I was in great shape at that time, and stayed like that up until 1972 or '73.

I used to train a lot on my own.

In the mornings at that time we'd be going to fairs as there were no cattle marts. We went to the fairs most days. You might be going off at three or four in the morning, but I'd run 10 miles before I'd go.

There was an old lady living down the road and she thought I was mad in the head!

I used to go down to the beach, which was about half a mile, and I'd run across the sand about three miles and come up another road parallel to our own and come back to the house. It was 10 miles to do the whole lot. I'd come home then in the afternoon after the fair and I'd be training again in the evening at the back of the house on my own.

I'd have the ball with me a lot of the time, but I used to like going out training. In the end I hated it – in 1974 and '75 I didn't really enjoy the training. But it definitely stood to me, and especially because of all the knocks I was getting. The work I did on my own would always stand to me on a Sunday in a game.

In 1964 Galway pipped us in Sligo, 2-12 to 1-12.

It was a good game but we were more disappointed to lose to them in 1965. The players were all going for that title and we had a great team, but Galway beat us in Tuam in '65 and they won the All Ireland that year.

Leitrim had beaten us in the first round in 1963 when we were hot favourites. They beat us by a point in Sligo – Packy McGarty was brilliant that day, he was brilliant all his life of course.

I was only one year in the corner and had moved out to the half-forward line by 1963. I preferred it out there, because you'd have more space there to get on the ball and you would get more shots at goal. You'd be roving the field more too; you were harder marked because you were moving all of the time.

I was In good shape so I could get around the place.

We were playing in the top division in the league and we fared very well over those years.

Another game I remember well is when we went to Rostrevor in County Down in 1968 when we were doing very well in the league. We needed a draw to progress – I was in charge of the team that time.

Barnes Murphy was missing so I brought John Brennan to centre-back; it was his first year with us because he was still a minor, and I brought in a lad from our own club, Andy Boland at full-back. He was playing on Sean O'Neill, who was one of the great players of the time. We beat them by a point.

We were getting a chance to play the top teams all the time – Down, Meath, Galway were the top teams in the 60s. We had their measure.

The team in 1975 that won the Connacht final was one of the weaker teams I played on. The three best years for Sligo when I was playing were 1970, '71 and '72. We had great players. Galway beat us after a replay in 1971; they lost the final to Offaly.

I don't know if we'd have done as well as Galway outside of Connacht but that was a very good Galway team.

Then, in 1965 we met Mayo in Charlestown.

We were six points down at half-time, and then nine points down immediately after. We started very poorly that day, but the whole thing changed later on.

We were six points down and a big lobbing ball came into the Sligo goalmouth in the first few minutes of the second-half and ended up in the net... so we were nine points down. Then we started to play well. I got a goal midway through the half and then Bill Shannon got a goal so we were right back into it.

Brendan McCauley and Bill Shannon at midfield were two good players. Bill Shannon maybe wasn't able for the hour but he had a good catch; he had a great pair of hands. He was so thrilled that day, because he was dropped in 1964 by Mayo and then he transferred to Sligo – so then to beat them in the Connacht semi-final was a big thrill for him. He was in GWI in Collooney, and he was a good addition for us but he was short term too, only two or three years. Joe Hannon was also a very clever footballer, he was there in the 60s.

I don't know if it was my goal or Bill Shannon's goal that turned it and did the most destruction, but it started to turn our way then after that.

I got a couple of great points from distance that day after the goal. I played on a lad that day who had played for Sligo in the earlier years. A man called Eamonn Walsh, he was from Charlestown. He played with Sligo first but then went to play for Mayo.

Anything could happen that time marking a man like that but Walsh was very clean. If he wasn't able to beat you fairly, he wouldn't try anything else.

We were still going well at the end of that match. It was great at the time to beat Mayo.

There were no papers at the time because the national papers were on strike, so no one reported on the game.

We started very well in the Connacht final against Galway.

Mickey Durkin was full-forward and got two goals in the first-half. We had them well rattled but we were playing with a bit of a breeze in the first-half. When we changed sides, the game was different and they won it by three points in the end. They were going for their second All-Ireland; they were beaten in the 1963 final by Dublin.

But we were well able to match them at that point.

I think I played my best football in 1970 and '71, I was going well in those years. I was doing a lot of the scoring because I was taking the frees. People would say you still had to score them but that was my job.

However, I didn't do much practicing with free-taking at the time.

I played 13 consecutive years with the province and it was a nice honour... and the Railway Cup was a very big thing that time.

When we won it in 1967 there were 50,000 people in Croke Park. The last number of years when it was on you wouldn't get 50 people at a game. To the likes of me, that was like an All-Ireland medal, and we got one again in 1969 but I came off injured that day.

I got on great with the Galway boys. And I shared a room with Joe Lyons who was at midfield that time for Mayo and Connacht. I was at his wedding actually too; we were good friends.

There were Cardinal Cushing games and trips to America as well which I will never forget. Langan from Mayo was on those trips. Christy Ring, the great Cork hurler, was on them too. They were a great experience and, believe it or not, Sligo were considered to be right up there with the other teams in those days.

I really enjoyed my football in the earlier years. By the time we won the Connacht final in 1975, I had lost some of the enjoyment because I was getting on. I wasn't going to play in '75 but Barnes Murphy kept coming out to the house and I eventually decided that I would.

But I was glad I hung on in the end.

We had a great club team as well in those years. We won the junior in 1964, so we had to go on our own then at senior level. Collooney Harps beat us in the final in 1965, and we were relegated again to junior.

We won the junior again in 1967 and senior in '68. We were beaten in the final in 1969, but won it in '70 and '71, and were beaten in the first round in '72… won it in '73 and '74. There were nine of the Connacht team playing in those Sligo county finals.

We played Collooney, who had a lot of the GWI lads including Bill Shannon, Brendan McCauley, and three or four Mayo fellas as well. Jimmy Killoran who played for Sligo and was in England for a while was on it too.

It shows how strong football was here at the time.

The football now is much better.

It's a different game, more of a running game. You see players passing back to the goalkeeper, across the field… that sort of stuff.

That would never have happened in our day.

The 2002 and '03 team was the best team ever we had in Sligo, I would say.

That was a great team. They beat Tyrone, drew with Armagh and they won the Connacht final. They were more balanced, probably a more level-headed bunch of men than our team. They trained hard and I thought they played some great games in Croke Park which I was so honoured to be a spectator at.

They were very proud days for me.

99

LIAM CAFFREY
(& BRENDAN McCAULEY)

GALWAY 1-12 SLIGO 2-6
Connacht SFC Final
Tuam Stadium
AUGUST 1 1965

Liam Caffrey and his teammates had the most powerful Galway team of all time to contend with in the 60s, but went agonisingly close to stopping them in 1965 in their winning tracks.

★ SLIGO: N Mullaney; P Keane, J Killoran, G McManus; S Durkin, C Cawley, **L Caffrey**; **B McCauley**, B Shannon (0-1); M Marren, D McHugh (1-1), M Kearins (0-3); J Hannon, M Durkin (1-1), N Farry. Sub: P Brennan for Hannon.

★ GALWAY: J Geraghty; JB McDermott, N Tierney, S Meade; J Donnellan (0-1), E Colleran, M Newell; M Reynolds, P Donnellan (0-1); C Dunne (0-5), M McDonagh (0-3), S Leyden; C Tyrrell (1-1), S Cleary (0-1), J Keenan. Sub: M Garrett for Reynolds.

THE ACTION

DESPITE LEADING BY seven points at one stage in the first-half, Sligo's record of coming up narrowly short in provincial deciders continued at Tuam Stadium when the reigning All-Ireland champions Galway escaped with a three-point victory.

Outplayed for the majority of the opening period, the Tribesmen came into the game having not played a single match in the province, owing to their tour of the United States. They were handed a bye into the final to accommodate their exertions across the Atlantic, where they beat New York in the league final.

On the other hand, Sligo came into the encounter in fine fettle, having overcome both Leitrim and Mayo. The win over Mayo, in particular, gave reason for much optimism heading into the county's first appearance in the Connacht decider since 1956.

Goals from Danny McHugh and Mickey Durkin in the first-half suggested Sligo's long wait for a second Nestor Cup success may be about to come to an end. With the underdogs seven points in front, 2-3 to 0-2, Sligo were in total control. In fact, their lead should have been more.

A clearly rusty Galway, playing into the breeze too, looked at sixes and sevens but eventually regained their composure. John Keenan's effort set up Christy Tyrrell for a soft Galway goal shortly before half-time, which cut the gap to four points, and turned the tie on its head.

The momentum was comfortably with Galway and with three quick points after half-time, Sligo's once significant advantage was now cut to a point.

Five points from Cyril Dunne, plus an industrious display from Mattie McDonagh, were among the highlights for the home side, but Sligo's midfield pairing of Brendan McCauley and Bill Shannon were comfortably on top for most of the hour.

Galway, somewhat wasteful at times, kept their noses ahead of the visitors for most of the second period and went on to end as three-point winners, despite Sligo's determined display.

Galway, of course, would go on to claim the All-Ireland again that September, and complete a three in-a-row in 1966.

★★★★★

"

IN 1965, I was into my final year in UCD, with exams in September.

During that summer, we had an educational tour to Europe… about 50 students. We went for two weeks or thereabouts, but before we were due home Sligo had to play Mayo in the Connacht Championship.

The tour of Europe started in Brussels and went right down to Italy and back again, on a bus over two weeks. The Friday before the Mayo game, I was due to fly from Germany to Dublin to be back in time for the match.

There were no direct flights that time from Germany to Dublin, so I had to go from Frankfurt to Brussels… to London… to Dublin. I went from Frankfurt up to Brussels anyway, and I got on a plane in Brussels which I thought was going to London.

I was on the plane a good while, but it turned out after a while that the one I was sitting on was going to The Congo!

Before the plane took off… a Caravelle jet it was… I was still very uneasy but at the same time I was convincing myself I was on the right plane.

A passenger came on and he said, 'You're sitting in my seat'.

I said no problem, 'I'll sit over on the next seat'.

The captain came down to enquire if something was wrong and to make a long story short he asked me if I was heading for Leopoldville.

'I hope not!' I replied.

The two planes were leaving the same exit so I had barely enough time to get on the right plane and got back on Friday evening to Dublin!

We had the match on Sunday and we were three points down with 10 minutes left in Charlestown against Mayo and we ended up winning by three points. It was a big result for us. We would have been doing okay in the National leagues but it was our first big win in the championship.

I had started playing junior football with Enniscrone/Kilglass back in the late 50s.

I went to college in St Muredach's in Ballina. We had no proper team except in my final year. We played in the Connacht Colleges Championship… I was captain but we were beaten. We played with all the Mayo lads and there was always a bit of aggro between the Sligo and Mayo lads… the Mayo lads were in the majority of course at the time.

Mickey Kearins was in there… he was two years behind me.

That time we had John Carey, Stanley Rowe and John Rowe on the Mayo team. Donal O'Grady was there too; he was a Mayo man but ended up playing with Cavan – he went to work up there and played with them for a good 10 years. Kevin Myles was another lad that played with Mayo.

We'd have internal leagues in the college. I was a boarder there. When you went in there to board there the only time you'd get home was at Christmas and Easter, even though I was only 12 miles out the road.

There was no real underage football at the time or no real football in national school, and whatever football we had was between ourselves in Carnduff or up in Quigaboy. In 1958 I played with a Tireragh team against Mullinabreena in the minor county final in Ballymote. It was a very good, competitive game but Mullinabreena came out on top.

I played minor football for Sligo in 1959. That time it was one game, no training… nothing, I didn't even know any of the lads except for Cathal Cawley, who was a cousin of mine. We got beaten in the first match… Mayo beat us in Sligo. We just scattered again and that was that.

After I finished in Muredach's I went to the Agricultural College in Mountbellew for a year and then I got a scholarship from there to go to Warrenstown College in Meath for another year. Then I went on to do a degree in Agriculture in UCD.

In Warrenstown we had a teacher by the name of Seamus Murphy, who had played midfield for Kerry; he won an All-Ireland or two. He used to play midfield with Mick O'Connell. He was training us there and he was a super trainer… he used to break up the crowd of lads into maybe two, three or four groups and he'd do all the exercises himself with each group; he was doing two or three times what everybody else was doing.

I never had any organised training before that at all… you would be lucky to get to the match on Sundays that time. You would be hoping for an early shower, because you might be making hay or something at home and if it was a good

Sunday you might not be able to go to the match… you'd have to do the work!

Always important to get priorities right!

In Warrenstown there was a Brother there… Brother O'Sullivan; he was on the Meath County Board and he was always hoping to get out to meetings and that, he was mad on football… a Kerryman. He used to do a bit of training with us as well. Sean Heslin was there at that time too, he used to play for Leitrim, and Brother O'Sullivan wanted Heslin and myself to declare for Meath so that he'd be able to bring us to the matches. We didn't go for it and he wasn't too happy.

Meath won the National League that year!

John Nallen, a great midfielder for Mayo and Galway, lived in Tuam for 12 years and won six or seven championships with Tuam Stars. He worked in the Ulster Bank and he was transferred up to Navan.

We had a challenge game one evening against Navan O'Mahony's. I was playing centre half-back. He'd just arrived and was going to play for Meath so there was a lot of attention and publicity about it. He had played inter-county for 10 years at that stage. He arrived anyway, and I was marking him on this particular evening, and nothing went right for him, and everything went right for me! I might add that one of my teammates that evening was Seán Boylan, who later became manager of Meath and won four All-Irelands.

When I started college in Dublin I played with Innisfree, a Sligo team in Dublin with all the Sligo lads together. A number of them played for Sligo later on but in the early stages we were playing junior football… we won the junior championship in Dublin, and then we went to intermediate and we got to the county final.

We played it before a Dublin vs Meath championship game in Croke Park. We were playing Scoil Ui Chonaill in the final and we got beaten by three points, in front of about 35,000 people. Jackie McHugh, Gerry McManus, Mickey O'Connor, Tommy Garvey, Gerry Garvey, Justin Henry, Peter Kildunne, Brother Hannan and Hugh McGonigle all played.

The club had formed just as I arrived in Dublin. Mattie Alcock, Peter Kildunne, Michael Haran, Joe Scully and a few others got it together.

I was with Innisfree when I got on the Sligo team.

Some of the Innisfree boys passed on my name after talking to some of the County Board lads. I was playing outside the county and not working in the county, so I had to declare for Sligo then, but I wasn't asked to declare until 1963, even though I was probably playing better football for the couple of years before that.

The first game that came up was against Leitrim in the championship in 1963. The year before, Sligo had run Roscommon very close; there was only a point or two in it at the end – Mickey Kearins had come on the scene too that time. The Leitrim one they reckoned was going to be an easy game for Sligo.

I was doing exams and had a tough exam on the Monday morning after the game so I didn't travel. As it happened, they lost by a point, so it was a bad start!

There was no organised collective training at that time. We would have National League games every second weekend, home and away. I was a college student, and Jimmy Killoran used to come from London and he'd hire out a car and bring down the Dublin-based players.

There wasn't a big difference between club and county; there was a bit of a step up but there was no big emphasis on training until 1965.

In 1964 we played Galway in Sligo and it turned out that year was the first of three All-Irelands in-a-row Galway won. They beat us by three points in Markievicz Park. It was my first Senior Championship game, although I played one Junior Championship match at centre half-back in Ballina against Mayo.

In 1965 the County Board brought in an Army man – Tommy Ryan, a captain in the army – and he came in to supervise the training.

He did a great job in the limited time available.

Galway won that All-Ireland in 1964, and they were on a tour of America to play the National League final in New York, which they won, and the Connacht Council gave them a bye to the Connacht final. We had to play Leitrim and Mayo to get into the final, and Mayo had beaten Roscommon.

Galway had no match before we played them.

We had fairly intensive training for about three weeks in Markievicz Park, mainly physical. There wasn't too much ball playing. I had come down for the summer and was staying in the Café Cairo.

I was studying there during the day and training in the evening. We were nearly training every evening. It was intensive but it was only for three weeks. The big thing before the game was David Pugh.

The ban was in force at the time, and Pugh had played international football for Ireland. He was a great athlete and was keen to play. He had been injured for nearly a year, hadn't played any soccer at all.

He came into training with us and he was great at the seven-aside because he had speed and control… he was a powerful athlete. He was going to be picked at centre-forward on the team and would have taken the pressure off Mickey Kearins.

On the Friday before the game, John 'Tull' Dunne of Galway rang Tom Kilcoyne, our county secretary, and he said, 'I hear ye are going picking Pugh and if ye do we are going to object… we know he played a junior soccer game and we've a vigilante who will bark and object if ye play him!'

He wasn't allowed play and I think he would have made all the difference on the day, a hell of a difference. When the ban was gone about five years later, he was able to come back properly and he proved what he could do.

Pugh not being there upset the plans because they were mainly based around Pugh and Kearins and how they would set up.

We turned up for the game in Tuam. They were a bit rusty in the first-half and we were seven points up with 10 minutes to go before half-time. They got a lucky auld goal that brought them back into the game. If we went in at half-time seven points up, it might have been a different story.

We had every confidence we could beat them, especially when they had no match. We had big men, 'good bulk' as the man says and they were in good shape. Shannon and McCauley were a great midfield pairing. Cathal Cawley was all bones, a solid reliable centre half-back. Mickey Kearins was probably the best forward in the country and he had good helpers in Mickey Durkin, Mick Marren and Danny McHugh.

I was marking Cyril Dunne.

I broke my ankle in that first-half, but at the time I thought it was only a sprain. I went in at half-time, and I tried to take the boot off but they wouldn't let me because I wouldn't be able to put it back on again for the second-half.

I played the whole game after. I was moving fairly badly in the second-half but I was doing the best I could.

Galway came back and beat us by three points.

It was a killer not to get over the line, and after that we met Galway in the Wembley Tournament. They had a full team, we had a full team… and we beat them in that and so we qualified for the game in Wembley in 1966, the year the World Cup was over there.

I wouldn't go so far to say we'd have won the All-Ireland if we beat Galway, but they did go on to win the semi-final against Down and Kerry in the All-Ireland final.

When you have the All-Ireland champions for three years ahead of you in the province it is a big problem. If we had a backdoor then we would have had a great chance.

I came back to play for Enniscrone/Kilglass in 1966 and we won the Junior Championship. When I finished college, I went to work in Donegal, in Raphoe.

It was 100 miles from home, and I'd come home to play the club games, though there weren't too many. It was nice to come home and win something.

My brother Aidan was captain that day.

In the 70s I was working in Kildare, I spent 10 years there. So, if we were going to a county match, I used to have to drive to Dublin to collect the lads, and go back again to Dublin to leave the lads back at home and down to Kildare again.

Sometimes when I'd come home for club matches some local lads might not even turn up! In 1972 Enniscrone/Kilglass played in the Senior Championship Final for the first time in something like 40 years. Barnes Murphy was captain and we got to the final against Curry. The match was fixed for mid-September.

This was a particularly hectic time for me as I was settling in to a new job, building a new house and preparing to get married in early October! The match did not go well for us – we were well beaten by a good Curry side which included five Colleary brothers.

They were great times playing football.

There used to be good craic going to the matches and that type of thing. For the league games with Jimmy Killoran, we used to go to the Roseland Ballroom in Mullingar or a marquee dance. In the period that I played with Sligo we were beaten in the championship twice by the eventual winners and once by the runners-up. In addition, we qualified for the semi-finals of the National Leagues on two occasions, in 1968 against Kildare when we got a draw followed by a defeat, and in '73 against Offaly. Another defeat.

I was selected on the Connacht team in 1968, but Ulster beat us in the semi-final. I was selected again in 1969 and we beat Ulster in the semi-final in Tuam. The final in Croke Park on St Patrick's Day was a big day that time. We beat Munster in the final, a team that included the great Mick O'Connell.

We won it and got a trip to America out of that. That was good. We'd all the top players in Connacht – there were five Sligo lads on it, Mickey Kearins, Peter James Brennan, Cathal Cawley, Jim Colleary and myself. We played New York in Gaelic Park and again in Boston in the Cardinal Cushing games. The aggregate score was a draw, so nobody won or lost. In 1970 I played again but we lost in the final.

It's great now to look back at all the great memories playing football. My final game with Sligo was in 1974 playing against Kerry at the opening of a pitch in Killorglin. I was marking Mick O'Dwyer in the first-half in what turned out to be his last game for Kerry and guess who came on in his place? The great Mikey Sheehy!

Enough said.

99

BRENDAN McCAULEY

Talented midfielder Brendan McCauley was spotted on the playing fields of London, and invited to offer his services to Sligo with whom he excelled even more.

66

I FIRST PLAYED for Sligo in 1958.

I was in The Brothers until 1957... I headed for London after my family had moved over and was there from '57. I think it was after the second game of football I played in London – it was a Roscommon man who got me to play with St Monica's – that Sligo came on the radar.

In that game, didn't I come up against Paddy Christie from Tourlestrane. I was marking him and somebody asked me afterwards what county I played with?

I said, 'No county... I don't play county!'

Then they asked me do I know who I was after playing on, and I said, 'No'. They told me it was Paddy Christie, and this fella said to me that he was the best man in London. I'd a good game on Paddy that day. They asked me would I like to meet Paddy, because he wanted to know what county I was from. I said I'd love to.

So, I told them I was from Cavan, but born in Sligo. Paddy asked me would I play for Sligo, and I thought sure how could I play with them and me living in London! But he told me they travelled over and back to play… so I said of course I will.

That's how it started… Paddy organised that the county would take me.

We travelled over and back for five years to play.

It wouldn't have been all that often; we weren't winning championships that time so if you got two championship games you'd have been very lucky. And we'd be back for a couple of league games too. There were four fellas – Jim Killoran, Paddy Christie, Brendan O'Boyle and myself.

I remember the first game… I was working in a bank then.

I used to cycle to work, so on the Saturday I cycled from West Ealing to Heathrow airport… 13 miles, put the bike up with no lock or anything and got on the plane. Then the next morning you'd be up at half four – we used to stay in Dublin and get the first flight back. But they were all at that.

Paddy used to have a motorbike. That time, it would cost my week's wages for the ticket, but the county would repay it later. That was one of the reasons why they asked in the end would I move home if they got me a job? And that's how it worked out. Peter Laffey was chairman around that time.

I was born in Strandhill and was only eight months old when we moved to Cavan.

I went to the Christian Brothers when I was 14… I took the bus to Dublin and was in there for about eight years. There were six years there where we were together, the whole group, and we played football every day. We very seldom missed a day.

And during the summer holidays we could play two or three games a day or play a game and walk to Portmarnock from Baldoyle… play around all afternoon… go for a swim… walk back and play another game in the evening!

It was a case of just picking two teams and into the game.

That's where I learned to play football. And it's about *playing* the game, you learn from making mistakes. That's my principle, and it remainded the whole way through afterwards. When I was training the minors, that principle was always there. Teach them what the skills are… catching, kicking, tackling… and then play the game. Those were the three principles that I believed in primarily.

Things improved for Sligo around the start of the 60s.

In 1962, I remember that Roscommon game and there was a lot happening, but Roscommon robbed us, and they went on to play Kerry in the All Ireland. Mickey Kearins got the goal, in his first game in championship coming up from minor. By the time 1965 came around, Galway would have been well ahead in the training and all that.

I would have done my training on my own. I'd be out on the road. In London, I was working nights in a job I was on and I used to bring the ball with me… going home in the morning I'd go into a big park at 6am and be kicking around!

I'd run the streets in London too after working.

I used to cycle. The first thing I bought in London was a bike. I used to cycle an hour or so to a certain spot, and I used to try and beat the buses to that point! It was just exercise, my way of doing it. But there was never any mention of training from the county; it was up to yourself.

We always had a good team with Sligo and we always felt we could deliver and do it. But we never really got together to work at it, to work on combinations and that. I remember, probably in that game in 1965, one of the forwards would jink one way or the other and I remember he gave an indication of the way he was going, so I kicked the ball… and he turned and went the other way!

That's the sort of stuff that could have been done in a training session… how to run and how to get the overall picture. And I would limit the solo run as well. The ball goes faster than anyone.

Galway had big names on their team, they were good. But in my mind, they were no different to me or any of our players; they didn't have any major stars.

Around the middle against Galway in a Connacht final was always difficult. They were all Connacht players, at that sort of level. Mattie McDonagh, John and Pat Donnellan… all those lads.

But we had quite a few players on the Connacht team in those years, including myself, Noel Mullaney and Cathal Cawley. Jim Killoran was a great footballer too; he used to come from London and played with us for a number of years.

And Mickey Kearins that day in 1965! I remember before the game started we were in a place in Tuam, having a cup of tea before we got to the pitch. I was standing at the door with Mickey, looking out at the street… watching the people going by and two or three were shouting things to us.

So I said, 'Come on, let's go up and sit down somewhere else!'

He got a lot of attention that day, absolutely, because they tried to put him off – they felt he was the one that could score and do the damage. In those days you could get away with it, but nowadays you'd be sent off.

I was thrilled with how we played in that final.

Pat Donnellan was at midfield; he was on me, and then they brought out someone else but I knew I had him. That's something else I could tell, when I was playing, when you felt you had the measure of your man.

I go back again to those Christian Brothers days. I was smaller at that time and used to have to play against somebody bigger and better usually, and I found that's where you learned to play; you found ways around it. Later on, I could tell when I had a fella and I could read the way he was going to move around.

That game, we had Mickey Durkin at full-forward, and he had Noel Tierney up the wall; he got everything that was going in there. They made a switch at half-time and put Bill Shannon into full-forward and brought Mickey out to join me at midfield. We had centrefield, and in fact in that game they brought out a third man, the corner-forward, to come out and help their midfielders. We had them that beaten.

In that 1965 match, the corner-back got me with his elbow into the side of my arm, and I played for the rest of the game after that happening in the first quarter, with my arm dead. I'd be using my other hand to lift the arm up to try and catch the ball. I couldn't feel it. I had no pain in it during the match but when we finished, it was awful. I had a mini at the time, and I had to drive to Galway after the match… and I couldn't move the gears with my arm. I went into the hospital with it then… there was nobody else to help.

People were disappointed afterwards when we lost but I was in Galway, I didn't even wait for a meal or anything after. I think we were disappointed that we were that close to getting over the line, against the All-Ireland champions. I absolutely loved playing football, and I really enjoyed my time with Sligo.

The club game was also played with real gusto, and you'd have as hard a game playing with the club as playing with the county. And it was strong too in Sligo – Collooney at that time had players and every one of them would have played for the county at some stage or other.

Bill Shannon was midfield with me with Sligo; he came to GWI way back in those days. And we also had Vincent Nally, another Mayo man; he ended up in Brooks Hanley and he was on the Collooney team with us in those days too. As was Mayo man John Morley.

John Morley played with Collooney Harps while working in GWI, but also played with Mayo (1961-74) and represented Connacht for many years. He later joined the Garda Siochana and rose to the rank of detective. He was tragically shot and killed along with a colleague, Henry Byrne in Roscommon following a bank robbery in 1980.

For me, playing, no matter what game I played, I enjoyed it, regardless of what came out at the end of it. Because that's the game, you can be as good as you want but unless lads are playing with joy… really loving the game, getting lost in it and getting stuck in and giving it one hundred percent… what else matters after all? It's a game of sport, and I think they are putting too much pressure on the players now.

They should be remembering that it is for the players, for the fun they get out of it, and when they're getting fun out of it, they will give their best. If they're thinking too much about it, it's going to interfere with their game.

That's why I think all the training should be around games and teams should work out their tactics in that environment. Now you have all the equipment and video and that. It's important to learn from it. You hear about teams now gathering for three or four hours a night – what do they get out of that?

I don't think it needs that time.

Players have homes to go to… and all the travel! That's all pressure, and every single person is different. You mustn't make it too serious; players have to live and get up the next day and get on with lives.

99

JIM COLLEARY

SLIGO 1-13 DERRY 1-12
National Football League Division Two Semi-Final
Irvinestown
MARCH 10 1968

Jim Colleary (second from right in the back row) had a consistency and accuracy up front for Sligo that earned him a call up to the Connacht team on a regular basis.

★ **SLIGO:** P Brennan; T McLoughlin, A Caffrey, D Martin; R Finnegan, C Cawley, L Caffrey; S Davey, B Murphy; M Kenny, **J Colleary (0-3)**, M Kearins (0-8); D McHugh (0-1), M Durkin (1-0), M Brennan (0-1). Subs: J Henry for McHugh.

★ **DERRY:** S Hasson; I Diamond, HF Gribben, M Kelly; M McAfee, H Diamond, T Quinn; L Diamond, T McGuinness; M Niblock (0-2), B Devlin (0-4), S Lagan (0-3); B Cassidy (0-1), A McGuckian (1-0), S O'Connell (0-2). Subs: C McGuigan for McGuinness, M Doherty for Hasson.

THE ACTION

SLIGO BOOKED THEIR place in the National League semi-finals with a hard-earned one-point win over favourites Derry at Irvinestown, Co Fermanagh.

With the league broken into eight groups of four teams on a regional basis, Sligo's progression into the next phase depended on the outcome of this encounter. Having finished second in their section – after wins over Fermanagh and Leitrim – Sligo were paired against 2B leaders Derry, with the winner set to play in the outright Division Two final for a place in the outright semi-finals.

Few would have expected anything other than a Sligo win at half-time, with the Connacht county running rampant in a wind assisted first-half. They held a 1-10 to 0-3 interval lead, with the goal coming from Tourlestrane's Mickey Durkin. Indeed, Sligo's forward unit enjoyed the lion's share of possession with Mickey Kearins and Jim Colleary registering 11 points between them over the course of the game.

Derry, however, were always going to fight back in the second period.

Sligo were forced to fight a rearguard action in a half dominated by a Derry side who were wasteful at times. Goalkeeper Peter James Brennan was forced into an outstanding save to prevent a certain goal from Colm McGuigan, while Sligo were also lucky to escape the concession of a second goal on a number of occasions in a frantic second-half.

With Sligo one point in front heading into added time, there were two final chances for Derry to earn a draw, but efforts from Brian Devlin and Sean O'Connell missed the target.

Sligo went on to beat Cavan to qualify for the outright league semi-finals at Croke Park, where they lost to Kildare after a replay.

★★★★★

"

THE MAIN THING that encouraged me growing up was watching St Nathy's, when they'd be playing their college games in the 50s and 60s in Charlestown.

They won an All-Ireland colleges in 1956, and had good teams in the years after and all of the great footballers that came off that. The likes of Mickey Durkin, Eoin Henry, Sean Durkin, Connor Maguire from Mayo, Colm Keane, John Joe Casey, Lukey Snee, Tommy Kilcoyne Anthony Haran... they were the ones that inspired us in school.

They'd be playing their games against Jarlath's, Muredach's and all the other colleges. It was a great standard.

The idea of training that time was only for the championship, there was no winter training, or facilities or anything like that. So, you got to know all the friends in the area at the time... Mickey Durkin, Jackie O'Hara, Peter James Brennan... all travelling down... Tom Roddy with the under-21's... the fun we'd have.

I played my football with Curry.

You'd play an under-16 game and then make up the numbers and tog out for the seniors, maybe go in at corner-forward or whatever. There weren't that many players around.

Curry were half a strong team, power-wise we had that but we didn't have the balance all the way through. We had Padraic Keane, Colm Keane and Noel Collins, and Sean Durkin was on the county team that time and was a stalwart... Paddy Doohan too. In the late-60s and 70s Eoin Henry kept the club going.

He held all the admin posts together. His wit and humour would get us out of any pickle.

'No funds?

'I'll ask Eamon to run a dance for us in the Central Ballroom!' (Eamon Walsh of Curry, Charlestown, Mayo and Connacht fame)

But that time it was just about getting together, there were no facilities or preparation, no training; you'd just turn up and play the game. It has changed greatly.

You'd do a bit at home training-wise – you'd be going to the bog, and back and forth, but physically you didn't need any of the gym work that they do now because you were working on a farm… you were fit. Look at the likes of Aidan Caffrey, he didn't need any training, all he needed was a bit of loosening out; he had the stamina, the speed, the power. He didn't have the semi-professional fitness of now but he, and everyone else, had 'agricultural strength'.

When I got onto the county senior team we had a lot of big men, no one was small. John Brennan, Liam Caffrey, Hughie McGonigle, Cathal Cawley, Robert Lipsett, Jimmy Kilgallon, none of them were small.

That was the style that time; you had to have a physical game, and referees allowed you to have a physical game.

There was no malicious intent in the tackling, it was just hard.

We played a county championship game with Curry against Collooney/ Ballisodare and that's how I got on for a challenge game at senior level against Kerry in 1966. I wasn't around for the championship as I was in England working for the summer.

The Kerry game was at the end of August, after Sligo were beaten by Galway in the 1966 Connacht Championship. They came up for a challenge. Kerry wanted to run out against Sligo to see how they'd fare against Galway. Sligo were regarded that time as one of the better teams; they were up there.

When you looked around at the likes of Cathal Cawley, he had a great delivery, easy for the forwards to pick up. Liam Caffrey the same, and we could hold onto at least forty percent of the play because of the good delivery from the half-backs. We didn't tend to bring in subs too often when the midfielders would get tired.

The midfielders had an awful lot to do in those days considering a player would only be fully fit in the summer period.

If you looked at the likes of Galway, they always had a player and a bruiser in midfield, that was their style. Mick Garrett and Donnellan had their time, the same with Jimmy Duggan when he had Willie Joyce with him… they'd always have a bruiser.

Kerry were the same, they'd always have someone in there for the physical stuff with Mick O'Connell, someone to do the breaking up of play and that.

Kerry in 1966 were strong.

I'd a good game. I was on Gerdi O'Connor and I well remember I won a hard fought ball and Mickey Kearins came over for a pass and I didn't give it to him and, of course, I didn't make much use of it after that. After that day, I always remembered if I had the ball to give it to him.

I didn't find the step up to senior football too bad because physically I was quite strong, but I well remember when I knew it was time to pack it up.

I was coming home from England for games and I played a game in Roscommon, and I set the ball out to Laffey on the right. I went for the return… hesitated.

I was a fraction late and I knew then that I wasn't playing good enough football in London. And that was it for me!

You have to be playing good fast football to stay sharp, you can't just expect it to happen. And also, when you're young, you'll make the nine or 10 runs anyway, but when you get older you might get a bit more protective and lazier, so I just knew then it was time to pack it up.

And then I gave up the club football.

Because, in all my playing career I wasn't afraid to mix it, but in all my time I learned that if you stand back from making a tackle, you'll get hurt. You're better to get stuck in; it's the same in hurling, they never hurt each other really because they tackle so close.

If you don't get into the tackle, you can get hurt.

I didn't play much in the summertime in 1967 as I was in England, but I was back for 1968.

The league was important for the county's finances, so there was an emphasis on the league. But it was very tiring, travel-wise and that. The travelling was tough from London in later years, but it was fun in its own way

The Derry match was my first game in the league. I travelled to it from college, from All Hallows in Dublin. There was some universities football that time, but before it was organised we'd have regular challenges with UCD; we had a good team.

It was so funny… Nick Clavin and I were in college together and we'd go in separate cars down to Crossmolina to play Connacht versus Leinster… then in separate cars back, after marking each other on the field!

You'd learn a lot from the colleges football.

But the hardest thing anyone on a football field has to get to grips with is the awareness of space. The top footballers that I have come across are the people who are very aware of space, and when they can be free. They know how to hurt you. That awareness is crucial.

Space is where the ball should be played to, but it isn't often enough.

We were going pretty well coming into that Derry game.

Everything was in place, the players were there. We put up a great first-half against them, and they couldn't come back. Danny McHugh was around at that time, playing well.

There were very good players who finished up early… Joe Hannon was another who was playing around that general period, but when some players were near the end of their days they were let retire, even though they might only be 30.

The same players were still good enough for a half, rather than a full game. They were classy players… Joe Hannon and Danny McHugh. However, the panels and the number of people travelling at that time were no bigger than 20.

The game was in Fermanagh. Someone picked me up from college to bring me down to it. There was a Sligo club in Dublin at the time call Innisfree – there'd usually be someone from Innisfree going to the game.

My preferred place was right corner-forward. But I started off at right half-forward, then corner-forward… then centre-forward, and midfield sometimes too. Against Cavan, in the following game, I was midfield.

Derry were a good team.

Sean O'Connell was playing for them. We were holding onto our lead – we had footballers in our defence at that time who could play… Cathal Cawley and Liam Caffrey. We were holding out.

We caught them on the hop in the first-half; we scored very freely. Then we had to defend seriously. I was back defending myself at the end and I got an elbow from Sean O'Connell in the mouth. But we'd get the ball and Mickey Kearins would be able to carry the ball a long way… and all we had to do was get a foul and maybe get the odd score… and slow it down.

There were no instructions or game plans… nothing.

There was never a game plan.

I'd get the ball and try and use it, and then follow it on… and try to use it again. I wouldn't hold onto it too long. You don't get a lot of time on the ball, so if you got it then you had to use it.

That's how I approached it. When you take too much out of it with the ball, you slow down everything – it allows the other team to fill up space in defence. Speed in getting rid of the ball always allows a team to create chances.

Then we had a tough outing against Cavan in the next game, when I adopted a tactic against Ray Carolan that I had seen. I had seen Des Foley tie up Ray Carolan. And I played him that way, with a dead hand… spoiling his run. I got bad reports about it… but anyway, that didn't matter! I decided to do a spoiling game on him because he was such a powerful man… you couldn't jump 50-50 with him.

There was great excitement after the Cavan game, which was very tough and physical because they were a good team at the time as well.

I enjoyed Croke Park.

We should have beaten Kildare the first day. This has always puzzled me… why did we not win replays in that period? I think it was down to tactical management – we were tactically naïve and not using substitutes. People didn't appreciate the value of subs at the time, that was my impression of it. There is always something in your head after a defeat like that. You always have something that nags away… always thinking you could have done something more or a little bit extra… something that might have made a difference.

They were always my thoughts on games like that which we might have won.

I was on the Connacht Railway Cup team for four years, which was a great experience. It was easy out there on the field sometimes because the players you were with were so good… like Jimmy Duggan. He was so elegant, you could read him a mile out.

I could always read Jimmy Duggan and get the pass off him and keep it moving on. It was like winning an All-Ireland medal when we beat Munster, and there were so many Sligo lads on it as well which was nice.

I have great memories and great friendships across the board from all of the teams I'd come across. As footballers, we respected each other, but we'd knock as many lumps out of each other as we could too. Like John Morley and myself.

When we played Mayo, he and I would go at it hammer and tongs. But the referee never took a name, never looked back at the pair of us. He knew it was 50-50.

To me, the friendships made through football were great. When we'd be travelling across the country for a league game, we'd pull up for a pit stop in Carrick-on-Shannon and we'd maybe meet the Meath team going home after a game against Mayo… things like that. We played a lot of games against Offaly in that period and we'd meet them maybe in Longford on a pit stop.

The football was tough but there was never a problem when we met up.

JOHN BRENNAN

SLIGO 3-5 MAYO 1-7
Connacht Minor Football Championship Semi-Final
Markievicz Park
JULY 5 1968

Winning the Connacht minor title in 1968 and going so close in the All-Ireland final is a summer of football John Brennan (pictured catching the ball in Croke Park) will never forget.

★ **SLIGO:** T Cummins; R Lipsett, **J Brennan**, N Kellegher; J Kilgannon, J Gilmartin, K Conway; A Richardson, D Kearins; K Carty, G Hegarty (0-2), H Quinn (1-2); R Sherlock (0-1), R Boland (1-0), P Kearins (1-0). Sub: P Ferguson for Carty.

★ **MAYO:** P O'Brien; F Hunt, F McGrath, D Mahoney; M Higgins, T McLoughlin, M Brennan; D Dolan, T Knight; T O'Malley (0-1), D Griffith (0-1), S Kilbride (0-2); F Burns, P Doherty (0-2), M Walsh (1-0). Subs: P Moynihan for Higgins, L McCann (0-1) for Doherty, K Durkin for Dolan.

THE ACTION

SLIGO PUT INDIFFERENT league form behind them to shock Mayo and progress to the Connacht minor football final.

A stylish and hard-working display from the home side meant they were deserving winners and probably should have won by more than the four-point margin. Indeed, the major difference between the two sides was evident right from the moment both teams hit the field, with a rugged Sligo outfit far more physically imposing than the visitors.

The first breakthrough for the home side came through the Tourlestrane combination of Aidan Richardson and Hughie Quinn, who combined for the latter to punch to the net in the early stages. Mayo responded in determined fashion and reeled off three points on the trot, before Mattie Walsh fired home a goal to put the visitors in front.

Peadar Kearins of St Patrick's made sure Sligo would lead at the break, however, when he netted before half-time to leave the hosts 2-2 to 1-3 in front.

In the 13th minute of the second-half Sligo made their decisive move with a third goal, scored by Richie Boland after he took a Richard Sherlock pass, and Mayo looked in all sorts of trouble.

Again, they fought back valiantly with three points in five minutes, including a Sean Kilbride effort, to edge closer. Sligo weren't to be denied, however, despite tiring somewhat in the closing stages, with Quinn registering their final point to send them through to the provincial decider.

★★★★★

"

MAYO WAS ALWAYS a big match for Sligo.

I'm actually living within 100 yards of the Mayo border, so I'm right beside it. My father, the house he lived in… half of it was in Mayo, so it was always a big match for us! To beat them always gave Sligo a big boost.

In the mid-60s Sligo had some brilliant teams… Mickey Kearins, the Caffreys, Cathal Cawley… they were all idols of mine at that time. Nace O'Dowd was gone before I came on the scene, I don't remember him playing. I've a vague recollection of Mullinabreena winning a senior championship in 1958, and he went to America then after that.

He was only down the road from where the pitch is now.

The first game I went to was in 1962… Sligo played Roscommon in Charlestown. I remember Mickey Kearins that time… he was only young, and watching him I always dreamed I'd play football for Sligo.

That's why 1968 is so special, it was my first time to play for the county… I got to live my dream.

The first time I played a game of football was in the vocational school in Tubbercurry. When I was growing up, there was very little underage football – actually there was no club in our area at the time. Mullinabreena had no club.

I played a little bit in national school – you'd play the local schools maybe a couple of times in the year – but the vocational school was the first real football I played. But I was crazy on football, from as early as I can remember. I'd even play on my own; I'd have teams in my head and I'd imitate Micheael O'Hehir commentating on games while I was playing! Mullinabreena came back into existence in 1966, and I got to play junior football.

In those days, it was a different football than it is now because every era has its own strengths and weaknesses, but I found it good and enjoyable.

I played a little bit in 1967 at minor level for Sligo. I was in the league team but I didn't make the championship team. I remember it well… to get playing was like winning the lotto. The selection for the county minor at the time was the decision of a representative or selector from each division.

In 1968, Walter Kivlehan was the selector from the south of the county, John

Gilmartin from Grange was from north Sligo, Eamonn Carney from St Pat's represented the west and Mickey Frank Regan then was from Keash in the east division. Colm Mullarkey was the manager with Brother Sebastian.

Colm was a man before his time; he was actually in the vocational school in Tubbercurry and that's where I learned a lot of my football, from Colm.

There was no real success at minor level before that for Sligo and, in fact, Mayo had been the main team. In 1966 they played in the All-Ireland and during that time they won five out of six Connacht titles. They were complete favourites – we played them on a Friday evening and we beat them well.

Training was very good. Colm Mullarkey was a very good trainer; he had great ideas. There was method to it too. It was very well organised. Our preparation was great... Colm and Brother Sebastian, they knew their stuff.

Personally, I was fairly fit anyway, because I was out farming all the time and I was naturally fit. We used to train three or four times a week. There'd be a lot of running and a lot of football too... we trained in Markievicz Park mostly, and we'd do a fair bit of ball work. There was a minor league in 1968 and we played four games... and lost the four of them.

But that team – the league team – was different to the championship one.

Lads from the vocational schools and that, they were the ones who played in the league, but then seven or eight players from the colleges would come in to training for the championship... from the likes of Summerhill. Those players came in and that made the difference.

But still, we had great confidence and belief.

Young lads are like that, and we really did have belief in ourselves. That belief and our ability brought us to an All-Ireland final where we were beaten by a point. It goes to show what can happen when you believe.

They were a great bunch of players... there were some brilliant players in the team. But still, coming up to the Mayo game, I don't think anyone in Sligo or anywhere else thought we'd beat them. Maybe Mayo were over-confident at the time too.

There was no talk about us. But we played the Sligo under-21 team the week before in a challenge match and we beat them well, and they were a fairly strong team. That gave us even more self-belief.

I was playing full-back. That year I played there all the time. When I started with the club, I played in every position but mostly in the backline. Most of the lads on our minor team were playing football with their clubs at adult level.

It was a good all-round team we had, we were all fit and strong. There were only two players under six foot on that team… everyone was well built as well. We were good footballers too, and we'd a very good midfield with Aidan Richardson and Dessie Kearins… they were fantastic. Before the game, we were togged out and all in Markievicz but… it turned out there were no jerseys!

I don't know what happened but there was some mix up. We ended up playing in Summerhill College jerseys, which we kept using after that. The County Board had jerseys for us but we stuck with the Summerhill ones… out of superstition! I'm nearly sure we wore them in the Connacht final, but once we got to Croke Park we wore the Sligo ones.

We started very well that night, and we were well ahead in the game.

Mayo had a lot of wides in the first-half, but we were completely on top of them from the start. Whether they were over-confident or what, I don't know. They came back into it a bit in the second-half but they never got ahead of us; we always managed to stay that bit in front.

It has happened before, Sligo teams losing leads, but thank God it didn't happen that evening! I remember the scenes after it well.

We beat Galway in the Connacht final, when we were big underdogs again, and then we beat Armagh in the All-Ireland semi-final.

Cork beat us in the final. We were 11 points down with 20 minutes to go and we came back… we got a penalty in the last few minutes to bring it back to a point. I still think if we got another minute or two, we might have gone ahead and won it, but that's the way it goes.

The scenes after the Connacht final were unbelievable… the last provincial win before that was in 1949 and actually Colm Mullarkey was playing on that team. But it's unbelievable to think that it hasn't been won since. There have been good Sligo minor teams over the years but they just could never get over the line, for whatever reason.

We definitely could feel that the win was important for the county. Sligo football was very strong at that time, even at senior. Right through the 60s, Sligo were able for the great Galway team in several games and played them in two Connacht finals, and were within a kick of the ball of winning one.

To get up to Croke Park was unbelievable.

I was 18 the day before we played Cork in the All-Ireland final. I had never been in Croke Park before, and had only seen the stadium on television, so the first time I was ever there was for that semi-final against Armagh.

It was easy to be in awe of it… even in those times it was a great stadium, it really was something else.

There was real excitement at the time. I'd be a cool sort of a person anyway, but it was something else to experience… for the county, for our families… it was a great occasion. The county really rowed in behind the whole thing.

It is great to look back and remember playing in the All Ireland final, but you also look back with a lot of regrets. We were very disappointed after it, definitely.

When you get that far and lose by a point, it's always going to be that way. And when we had the chances to win it as well in the end, that makes it a bit tougher. Cork got three goals in the first-half and one or two of them they shouldn't have got, but anyway, you'll always have regrets when you lose a big game.

We got a civic reception in the Town Hall when we came back.

I've a real memory of Noel Kellegher, who was a corner-back, crying and going over to the Lord Mayor and apologising to him for losing the final. It was actually Noel who scored our penalty.

People took a lot of pride in our comeback in Croke Park – and then there was the very sporting gesture afterwards when Aidan Richardson and Dessie Kearins carried the Cork captain off the field, which was something you very seldom saw.

I had never seen it before and I have never seen it since. It was an iconic moment. At senior level I'd think of 1971 especially, when Galway beat us in a replay in Castlebar. There were some great footballers on that team and Mickey Kearins was in his pomp in '71 – in '75 he was still good but he was probably past his best days. Definitely we could have won either of those games, and Galway went on to the All-Ireland final that year where Offaly beat them. We played in a few league semi-finals, and got beaten in two of them – Roscommon beat us in one, Offaly beat us in the other.

If we got out of Connacht around that time, I think we would have been there or thereabouts for an All-Ireland title. In 1975, I don't know what happened.

People say the 1975 team was old but it wasn't really, there were only a few older players on it. We were in the game for a long time against Kerry that day but things went awry in the last 10 or 15 minutes.

We thought we were good enough and I always personally believed that we could be good enough, that we definitely would be there or thereabouts. You'd always dream about winning All-Irelands.

My minor memory is a little bit sweeter than my 1975 memory at senior level.

Growing up and watching Sligo teams do well in the 60s, it was a dream that I'd play some day for the county and getting the opportunity to play minor was a first big break, as they say, so that's why I'd have a special memory for that one. But I have a lot of good memories of a lot of games I played in – and bad ones too!

I enjoyed it immensely; we'd some great times and we'd travel on buses all over, and up to the North. That time we'd travel up to Derry and Down a lot and we had some great trips up there and good games too, very enjoyable.

Football back then… to see it back now on videos it looks terrible, but to me it was more like football really. I know people might not agree, and I know it has moved on completely with the speed of the game and the amount of time and effort that players put in now… it's nearly a professional thing. But as I say every era has its strengths and weaknesses.

There were seven or eight of the minor lads that played senior for Sligo in the early 70s, and in 1975 there was four from that minor team that played – Tommy Cummins in goals, Robert Lipsett and myself, we were corner and full-back, and Dessie Kearins was the other one… we were the four in '75.

And the funny thing is there's only four players in the county who have a minor Connacht and a senior Connacht medal, and two of them – Robert Lipsett and myself – were two Mullinabreena players, so we're unique in that sense anyway

"

MATTIE BRENNAN

SLIGO 3-10 GALWAY 1-17
Connacht SFC Final Replay
Tuam Stadium
JULY 25 1971

Like many on the 1975 Connacht title winning team, Mattie Brennan believes Sligo had an even greater shot at All-Ireland glory four years earlier.

★ **SLIGO:** T Cummins; J Gilmartin (0-1), J Brennan, A Caffrey; **M Brennan**, C Cawley, J Kilgallon; T Colleary, S Davey; D Pugh (1-0), J Colleary, M Kearins (0-7); G Mitchell (2-1), P Brennan, H Quinn (0-1). Sub: A Richardson for Davey.

★ **GALWAY:** PJ Smith; B Colleran, J Cosgrove, N Colleran; L O'Neill, T Gilmore, C McDonagh; L Sammon, W Joyce (0-1); J Duggan, J McLoughlin (0-4), M Rooney; E Farrell (0-1), F Canavan (0-4), S Leyden (1-7). Sub: M Feerick for Rooney.

THE ACTION

SLIGO ENDURED ANOTHER near miss in their search for that elusive Connacht title in late-July when they came up so narrowly short against Galway in this replayed decider.

After playing out a 2-15 apiece draw in the original fixture at Castlebar's MacHale Park – with Mickey Kearins producing an outstanding individual display in registering 0-13 – Sligo could have won this game.

David Pugh's late goal put a closer reflection on the scoreboard than perhaps was the case throughout the course of the second-half, but the opening half showed Sligo meant business.

Two goals from the boot of Gerry Mitchell – both Mitchell and Pugh, Sligo's goalscorers, were in action for the county following the removal of the controversial ban on soccer players participating in county football earlier that year – ensured Sligo not only kept pace with the hosts, but actually led by a point on three occasions throughout the course of the first 40 minutes.

Trailing by a point at half-time, 1-9 to 2-5, Sligo were back in the ascendency early in the second-half after two Kearins frees, but Galway would soon power on.

While Kearins was Sligo's outstanding player, Galway's own marksman Seamus Leyden was also in good scoring form, notching up 1-7 – while Liam Sammon was among those most effective in the middle third.

Sligo battled hard, yet Galway's four-point lead saw them in a comfortable position heading into the final stages. That was their advantage after midfielder Willie Joyce – arguably the Tribesmen's best player – pointed in the 75th minute, but Pugh's late, late goal brought Sligo to within a point.

So near, yet so far for a Sligo team that was rated as among the best the county ever produced.

★ ★ ★ ★ ★

66

IT WAS A huge achievement to win in 1975 and we were so lucky to have a Connacht title, but I think if we'd made the breakthrough in '71, especially with David Pugh and Gerry Mitchell having just joined the team, we could have gone further. If the two lads had got a chance of playing more games, they'd have only got better. They were hugely talented. Mitchell was a great poacher, and Pugh was so physical and strong.

I've chosen the 1971 Connacht final replay as my most memorable game because it was the day I established myself as a half-back on the Sligo team. Before then, from back in 1967 when I played my first senior game for Sligo in a Gael Linn match, I was in at corner-forward.

That first game, I'd have been lost in the inside forward line without the help of my clubmate Mickey Durkin, who was beside me at full-forward. He kept encouraging me to take my own score but, to be honest, I hadn't the confidence… or the accuracy! So I was only too glad to get back to the half-back line in 1971.

From then on, I wore the No 5 jersey with Sligo till 1983 and '84, when I played a few games at corner-back.

In 1967, my last year at minor level, I was honoured to be captain of the first team from Tourlestrane to win a Minor Championship. I'd been playing senior for Tourlestrane since the age of about 15. Emigration was rife in those days, and numbers were low.

I also played minor for Sligo for four years, and Colm Mullarkey was a huge influence in those early playing days. In 1968 he brought the minor team to the All-Ireland final, a brilliant achievement. Unfortunately, I was overage by a year.

In my last game at minor level, the year before in 1967, we played Mayo in O'Hara Park, Charlestown. Things didn't go well. We got off to a bad start and the game just ran away from us. It was an eye opener for me and I learned a lot that day. I'd been dominating at centre-back those years as a minor, but Mayo were able to drag me out of position and it really worked. I never got into the game properly.

In the 60s the Sligo team was formidable.

We got to a league semi-final in 1968 against Kildare when I was 18. As I've said, I was playing corner-forward, but I was dropped for the replay. Looking back, we were there or thereabouts in the late-60s but never had a killer instinct. But it was a great introduction to the county team for me, and my new teammates were very supportive. I'm thinking of the late Cathal Cawley, Mickey Kearins, Mickey Durkin, Peter James Brennan (RIP) and the others.

In 1971, we played the first game of the championship against Roscommon. They were a good team at the time, but I always felt we could match them. We never feared them. We beat Roscommon, so then we were into the Connacht final in Castlebar against Galway. We drew with them in the first match, but we could already tell Mitchell and Pugh were a great addition to the team.

It's funny… Sligo was one of the last counties to maintain support for the soccer ban and yet was one of the first to allow the soccer lads to play.

Between that first day and the replay, there was huge excitement all over the county… absolutely huge, it was palpable. I remember the replay clearly.

I was marking this young Rooney lad, who was supposed to be a star for Galway. But actually I played well that day. It was a close game the whole way through. We had a chance to level things towards the end when Pugh took a '50', but the ball drifted wide.

Galway were a very strong outfit. They'd the likes of Seamus Leyden, Liam Sammon and Willie Joyce, who were well renowned players. For us, Kearins was flying in those matches, kicking massive scores. Kearins was class.

He was by the far the best footballer in the country at the time, I think… the best of the lot. With Pugh and Mitchell in form as well, we'd a team that could match any other.

We'd a strong backline that day, too. Jimmy Kilgallon had just joined the team and was a really promising player, but, unfortunately, he got injured later in the year and didn't play much after that. John Gilmartin was an excellent footballer. Cathal Cawley, the Lord have mercy on him, was outstanding. He was as hard as nails. He wasn't a dirty player, but he was such a tight, strong marker. A very physical man, but the type of character who'd walk through you one second and give you an apology for it the next.

And another thing I remember about Cathal is that all the young lads, myself included, would be rushing for sets of togs and socks before games. We'd have the wrong socks with us or maybe no socks at all.

Cathal was always the man to sort us all out with gear.

Tourlestrane had three lads playing with the team that year... Hughie Quinn, Aidan Richardson and myself. Paddy Henry, a close neighbour and friend of mine, joined the team later that year.

But you can imagine the hurt not to have got over the line that second day against Galway.

Especially, I think, in south Sligo. We used to claim it was the home of football in the county, and everyone around the place was so disappointed.

In terms of the training leading up to that match and around that time generally, it was nothing compared to today. We thought we were working hard at it, training two or three nights a week. But the commitment lads have to give now is on a different level to what we had to do.

In 1972 we drew with Mayo in the first round of the championship and were beaten after extra-time in the replay in Castlebar. That was another major disappointment.

We were lucky, I suppose, to win a title in 1975.

It could have passed us by. I'm sure many people thought we'd missed our chance in 1971 and '72. To win a Connacht title was a massive boost for Sligo. I think the influence of Barnes Murphy in 1975 as player-manager was huge.

It was his leadership that got us through.

But in the All-Ireland semi-final, Mick O'Dwyer's Kerry were at a different level of training and coaching. I think that made all the difference. Before the game, I was told to watch Mickey Ned O'Sullivan and keep him out of the game. He was a young fella with a mighty reputation. It was a bit of a non-event for me, though, because while I kept him out of the game, I was out of it myself as well!

Sligo were in Division 1 in those days and the RTÉ commentators rated us highly. They were interested in getting interviews with us. I remember Micheal O'Muircheartaigh asking how come we never pushed on after that title in 1975.

But we didn't; we went back after that year.

As I've said, I still believe that if we'd won a Connacht final in 1971 we could have made it to an All-Ireland final that year. Croke Park would have suited us.

Pugh and Mitchell would have had the chance to become even more influential, and we'd great pace in the team… we would've loved the big pitch.

I've great memories of my playing days for Sligo. The fellas who were there when I was coming onto the senior team… Liam Caffrey, Cathal Cawley, Mickey Durkin… all of them, really, they were so welcoming. Brendan McCauley was great, too.

I worked in GWI at the time and he was there as well, and he'd come over and have the chat and give me encouragement. The late Peter James Brennan was another mighty friend, and so were the likes of Johnny Stenson (R.I.P.), Tom and Jim Colleary, Paddy Henry, Tommy Carroll… all the lads.

We had so many great and memorable match days, some brilliant experiences. It was a privilege to play with those fellas and in those teams.

PADDY HENRY

MAYO 2-7 SLIGO 0-12
National Football League Division One B
Crossmolina
DECEMBER 12 1971

Paddy Henry (second from right) served Sligo with equal distinction up front and in defence for almost 15 years.

★ **SLIGO:** T Cummins; L Caffrey, C Cawley, A Caffrey; M Brennan, T Colleary, J Kilgallon; S Feeney, H Quinn; **P Henry**, J Colleary, M Kearins (0-9); F McCarrick, PJ Brennan (0-3), D Connolly. Sub: P Kearins for Kilgallon.

★ **MAYO:** JJ Costello; K Lavelle, J Morley, R Niland; M Begley, J Carey, T Keane; S O'Grady, M Higgins (0-1); M Sheridan (0-2), S Kilbride, P O'Dea; P Glavey, F Burns (1-1), JJ Cribbin (1-2). Sub: J Corcoran (0-1) for Glavey.

THE ACTION

SLIGO'S FINAL GAME of an eventful calendar year in 1971 ended in disappointment at Crossmolina, with Mayo taking advantage of the visitors inefficiency to run out as one-point winners.

After a heartbreaking Connacht final saga, which ended in a one-point replay defeat to a Galway side who went on to contest the All-Ireland final, Sligo were back into league action in Division 1B.

Approaching the game after a reversal against Meath in Navan two weeks previously, the Yeats County handed a debut to Tourlestrane youngster Paddy Henry at wing forward.

The game is also remembered for the wrong reasons. A serious knee injury to wing back Jimmy Kilgallon – a member of the famous 1968 minor side which went so close to All-Ireland glory – ended his involvement after little more than 20 minutes.

Like many of their encounters against Mayo and Galway in this era, this was a game Sligo could have won. They kicked 15 wides, and still had a good chance to level the game when Hughie Quinn's late attempt went inches wide.

However, 0-5 apiece approaching half-time, Mayo, with the aid of the breeze in the opening half, made a decisive move.

JJ Cribben's outstanding goal was the major difference, and helped the home side lead by 1-7 to 0-5 at the break, with Sligo's first-half scoring exploits dominated by Mickey Kearins, who registered 0-9 in all.

Sligo battled hard in the second period to retrieve the deficit and were well served by full-forward Peter James Brennan, who was on hand to supply three points from play, while Kearins remained a constant thorn in Mayo's side.

However, Mayo – beaten finalists in the 1970 league final – hung on to claim victory, despite a valiant effort from UCD student Hughie Quinn in the final moments which agonisingly went past the upright.

★ ★ ★ ★ ★

"

IN LATE NOVEMBER 1971, I went with my friends Donal Brennan, Mick Marren and Frank Kilcoyne to support Sligo playing Meath in Navan in the National League. Sligo did not play well and lost.

Two weeks later, Sligo faced Mayo in Crossmolina and instead of looking on, I was selected to play at wing forward despite not having any connection with the panel prior to that.

A friend told me that he had heard on the evening sports news that I had been selected and, later in the week, Tommy Kilcoyne informed me, by post, of my selection and the travelling arrangements. Naturally, as an 18-year-old, it was very exciting to be selected – it was always a dream to play county with Sligo.

That it happened so quickly was due to my club Tourlestrane and my school St Nathy's Ballaghaderreen. From the mid-60s to the mid-70s Tourlestrane was very strong at underage level, often contesting finals with Muire Naofa. I was involved in four minor finals, three of which we won from 1967 to '71. We had some exceptional young players, like Aidan Richardson, Hugh Quinn and my neighbour Mattie Brennan. Amazingly, he played minor championship for four years, which must be a record in this county.

Mentors like Mickey Gallagher, Nace Feeley, Jon Durkin and Joe Storey helped us greatly to progress. Now I was following in the footsteps of the aforementioned players.

Luck was on my side too in that my years in St Nathy's coincided with a very successful period for the college. In 1968, we won all three Connacht titles and my football heroes in school were Sean Kilbride, Mel Flanagan (the well-known golf coach) and clubmate Hugh Quinn. Two of my classmates John O'Mahony and Con Moynihan won All Ireland minor medals with Mayo in 1971, but I had failed to shine for Sligo at minor level.

Yet six months later I was about to make my Sligo debut against Mayo, as was Seamus Feeney from Grange at midfield.

I travelled to the game with Mattie Brennan, Hugh Quinn and our driver Liam Caffrey from Dublin; a long drive but standard procedure at that time. I was walking into a dressing-room to play with men I had been watching for years...

Mickey Kearins, Tom and Jim Colleary, Peter James Brennan, John Brennan, Barnes Murphy… the Caffrey brothers. They had lost the Connacht final after a replay to Galway six months earlier.

The Mayo dressing-room included Sean Kilbride, John Morley and Tom Fitzgerald, the latter two often trained with us in St Nathy's. John was a Garda in Ballaghaderreen at that time.

My direct opponent was Tom Keane from Claremorris, but after 20 minutes I found myself at left half-back as Jimmy Kilgallon suffered a serious knee injury. His injury in many ways decided where I was to eventually play my football with Sligo. Kilgallon's injury was a huge blow to Sligo football as he was a really special player.

My memories of the game are very hazy now, but as usual Mickey Kearins was on song scoring nine of our 12 points. I also recall Hugh Quinn having a very narrow wide at the death to level matters.

Personally I hoped that I had done enough to keep my place for the post-Christmas matches.

For the following two years I alternated quite a bit between defence and attack, but invariably for the crunch games I was in the half-back line with Mattie and Barnes. I got the 'utility player' tag. As a friend reminded me… 'That just means you are useless in more than one position!'

Mayo were the opposition again for my championship debut in June 1972.

This ended in a draw in Sligo, and a thrilling replay in Castlebar. It was probably the most exciting match I recall from my Sligo years, as it went to extra time. The physicality of the exchanges was several degrees higher than National League fare and on a roasting hot day I had to come off at half-time in extra time due to sheer exhaustion.

Mayo won, but three years later in similar circumstances we had our revenge to win the Connacht final.

My early years with Sligo were far more successful as we contested the National league semi-final in both 1973 and '74, and the All-Ireland semi-final in 1975. Being in Division 1 of the league meant quality games against teams like Derry, Tyrone, Down, Mayo… Meath – and Sligo was very competitive in that company.

In my later years, things had changed; now Fermanagh, Waterford, Tipperary,

Clare and Wexford were our opposition as we found ourselves in Division 3 and 4. I recall going by bus to play Kilkenny and then manager Mick Breslin telling me somewhere in Carlow he was resting me for that particular game. I have a soft spot for Carlow ever since!

On Carlow… one of the best players I ever played with was Carlow dual star Cyril Hughes, a Railway Cup winner with the Combined Universities in 1973.

Of course, in a county career with Sligo there will probably be more disappointments that highlights or so history tells us. Games I recall for that reason include the 1973 loss to Galway in Tuam, the National League semi-final loss to Roscommon on my 21st birthday, my poor display on the day we won the Connacht final in '75, and the championship defeat to Leitrim in '79 when I was captain.

I prefer to remember the highlights; playing in Croke Park in the semi-final of a national competition in three consecutive years from 1973 to '75, beating much fancied Roscommon in '81; representing the Combined Universities and Connacht, and being chosen to travel as a replacement with the All Stars in May 1976. This gave me the opportunity to play with and against top footballers from every county, which I greatly enjoyed.

Then there's always the funny side-shows and meeting people you would never have thought possible.

Dave Bacuzzi, for instance, was the very successful manager of Cork Hibs and Home Farm soccer teams in the 70s. In November 1975 I found myself in Tolka Park at a Home Farm training sessions asking him to introduce me to Trevor Endersen, later physio to the Irish soccer team.

I was trying to recover from a very serious injury – a severed muscle in my thigh – and a chance meeting with Kildare footballer Eamon O'Donoghue led to a possible solution.

Against my better judgement I had lined out for Sligo in a challenge game against Roscommon, despite having played four games in a third level nine-aside tournament in Dundalk RTC the previous day. Inside five minutes, the muscle snapped and put me out of action for five months.

Endersen told me that I should have had surgery to reattach the muscle the following day but that it was now too late. He set me up with a programme for the gym in St Pat's in Drumcondra that got me back to fitness.

I also may be the only Sligo player to have played for a team managed by Big Tom!

Visiting a college friend from Oram, I went with him to a tournament match against a club from Tyrone. Oram were short of players and Big Tom tapped on the car window and suggested I join my friend in the Oram dressing-room. Not only had Big Tom donated their playing pitch, he was also team manager that particular year.

My instructions were simple… 'Don't say anything during the game because your accent could get us into trouble!'

And so I played in total silence and we won!

Musically, however, I remained steadfast in the Chuck Berry camp!

Looking back to 50 years ago, the realities of county football then were very different from those of today. Collective training only happened for a few months prior to the championship. There was no gym work because the facilities didn't exist, and nutrition was a word only used in hospitals.

And, unlike Dublin today, we didn't bother too much with… 'Following the process!'

Players did their best individually to keep in shape, to represent their county well and to have plenty of fun and laughter along the way. I certainly did over the years with Sligo from my debut in December 1971 to my final game in Carrick-on-Shannon versus Leitrim in June 1985, a game in which I was deservedly substituted in the second-half.

Walking along the touchline I knew it was time to go.

And by the time I reached the dugout, I had retired.

MATTIE HOEY
(& BARNES MURPHY)

SLIGO 2-10 MAYO 0-15
Connacht SFC Final Replay
MacHale Park
JULY 20 1975

Mattie Hoey scored four vital points when Sligo travelled to Castlebar to finish off the job against Mayo in the Connacht final in 1975.

★ **SLIGO:** T Cummins; R Lipsett, J Brennan, T Carroll; M Brennan, **B Murphy**, P Henry; J Stenson (0-1), T Colleary; M Laffey, **M Hoey (0-4)**, F Henry; D Kearins (1-1), M Kearins (1-4), J Kearins. Sub: B Wilkinson for Laffey.

★ **TEAM:** J Heffernan; J O'Mahony, S Reilly, TJ Farragher; G Feeney, C Moynihan, M Higgins (0-2); F Burns, D McGrath (0-3); T O'Malley (0-4), J Keane (0-1), E Webb (0-2); W McGee (0-1), S Kilbride (0-1), G Farragher (0-1). Subs: J Cultin for O'Mahony, M Higgins for Burns.

THE ACTION

YEARS OF TOIL and effort, only to fall so narrowly short on several occasions, finally culminated in silverware for Sligo as the county bridged a 47-year gap to capture the Connacht Senior Championship title.

Indeed, many in the lead up to this encounter may have thought that Sligo had let their chance at glory slip once again in the original fixture, which ended in a draw at Markievicz Park a fortnight earlier. At one stage, the Yeats County held a six-point lead but at the finish they were fortunate to escape with another shot at glory.

This time, they made no mistake, though it certainly was not plain sailing.

Mayo, on home turf, held the upper hand for long stages on a hot July afternoon. In a game that stood out for its hard tackling, the hosts established a 0-9 to 0-7 half-time lead and looked comfortable as the game progressed towards the closing stages.

Sligo needed a lift from somewhere and got it in the shape of two goals.

The first came from the penalty spot after Mickey Kearins, fouled initially by Seamus Reilly, dusted himself off and dispatched a superb effort into the roof of the net to put Sligo 1-7 to 0-9 in front.

Sligo still fell 0-13 to 1-8 behind as the game headed for the final quarter but a superb team move, started by a good fetch in the middle by Tom Colleary, saw Kearins turn provider as he knocked the ball down into the path of Des Kearins, who rattled a shot to the corner of the net, and put Sligo in front again.

Tense moments were the order of the final stages, but Sligo managed to keep their noses in front. The final whistle was greeted with scenes of great joy as the Yeats County, after so many years of heartbreak, finally reached The Promised Land.

Barnes Murphy hoisted the Nestor Cup aloft amid scenes of great jubilation, which continued as the team returned to a heroes welcome in Sligo.

★ ★ ★ ★ ★

"

THE FIRST TIME I played championship football at senior level was at inter-county level with Sligo in 1975, as we only had a junior club in Grange. I made my debut in 1974 versus Tyrone in Tyrone.

When I was growing up, back when I was seven or eight, at the homeplace we had a shed beside it with a door on it. I'd spend every evening there banging a ball off that, from all angles, so when I went out to play a game or anything like that, I felt like I could put it through the eye of a needle.

It definitely stood to me playing football at senior level.

I was born and reared into football. My father played football, my brothers played football... we all played GAA. My father was telling me one time how big it was around Grange village once upon a time, way back in the day when you had 13 local teams. That'd mean nearly every townland around the village had a football team.

It was all GAA back then.

I started in the national school and as soon as we got in we started playing football with the school, when I was able to get onto the team with our teacher in Grange NS Aidan McGowan (RIP). He was later president of the Connacht Council when we won the title in 1975.

Moving on from national school, I played at all levels with Grange and then I attended the tech in Grange... the vocational school. We'd a teacher there called Mr Ford – Eamon Ford, who was a Clare man. At that stage, when we were playing the vocational schools football it was a big thing back then.

He would draw the game out on the blackboard for us... he'd take us into a room and draw it out. The only man I saw doing that again was another Mr Ford, when I was involved with Sligo in 2002 along with Peter Ford.

So we were playing football the way Kerry played football in 1975, when I was with the tech in Grange. An example of that was when we played Coola, and we were doing the Inter Cert and they were doing the Leaving Cert. They had, I think, seven or eight fellas on the county vocational schools team and they were two years older than us.

But we still beat them, after a replay, to win a final way back then.

In 1975 when we won the Connacht final I was only a junior footballer, playing with a junior club, but I also played with Dundalk Regional College. I got an apprenticeship with the ESB and that's where we did our three months every year, in Dundalk, so I was playing football for them and we would have played in Croke Park.

We won what would be, I suppose, the equivalent of the Sigerson back in the day, though it wasn't called Sigerson back then… I think it was called advanced colleges; that was back in 1973.

I played at midfield along with a fella called Jimmy Kirk from Dundalk, and our opposition on that day was Bobby Miller of Laois and Leinster, and a man called Matt Gilsenan from Monaghan, who actually ended up being my next-door neighbour in Grange years later!

It was a serious level to be at, even though I would have played minor with the county and captained the under-21 team.

I didn't find much of a change moving to inter-county; football was fairly natural. The better the footballers you played with, the easier it was to play football.

Even later on in life in the ESB, we won seven or eight inter-ESB things and we actually had a team where we had Willie Joe Padden and Anthony Molloy at midfield for us on an ESB team… and we'd James McHugh and Barry McGowan, lads with All-Ireland medals.

History will tell you we haven't won a minor title in Sligo since 1968. I played two years at minor, around 1971 and '72. We wouldn't have been that strong, but later at under-21 level when I was captain of the team we were beaten by Mayo, I think in Ballyhaunis, and I think Barnes Murphy was the manager of the team.

I was playing midfield that day; we scored nine points and I got seven of the nine from midfield.

At underage level with the club I used to play midfield or centre-forward. But I played a lot of football with a lot of different teams, and I'd say over the years I must have covered nearly every position on the field! But centre-forward was a lovely position to be playing because you could dictate the way the game went, the way the passes went and all that.

In 1974 versus Tyrone, in Tyrone, was my league debut for Sligo.

I wasn't expecting to be called in, there wasn't really any expectation that time.

It was a case of if you were called in, *you were called in*. My good friend Seamus Feeney also played in that game – we both played midfield together for the club.

That time it was just *play* football… and that was it.

I don't remember much from the debut in 1974. There wasn't really that much of a change physically, if you could see what was coming.

You could read tackles or see the boot coming in and all that; you'd be able to deal with it. You would get a lot of attention off the backs. When I think back to some of the full-back lines, they would put the studs down the back of your leg straight away.

And they'd get away with it at that time, in addition to a lot of pulling and dragging and that stuff. It's only later on in years that good movement came into the games.

Before I started playing myself, we'd have gone to all the county matches; there was a neighbour down the road, Francis Branley (RIP) who used to bring us to all the matches. We'd go down the road and ask him to give us a lift to the game; he'd bring us to every match.

I don't think there was much in-depth thinking about the football at that stage when I came into in 1974 or '75, it was just about doing a bit of training and playing the game – there'd be no stats or any of that craic at all!

But Sligo were keeping up with the best teams at the time.

Mickey Kearins was probably the best forward I played with. All you had to do was find him in a half yard of space and he'd finish; all you'd have to do was get it onto him. He was a genius.

Any man that scored 10 or 11 points in Connacht finals in the 60s and then not to win one, it must have been heartbreaking for him.

The atmosphere in the team was very good in 1975.

You'd make great mates, everyone was trying really hard and everyone would do their best to win games. There wasn't much in-depth thinking to it – you know the way they go on now with goals and all of this, they'd blow the head off you now with stats and all that craic. And still, when you look at the scoreboard at the end of the game, that decides who wins!

The form of the team heading into 1975 was good enough, but we lost a few games in the league. We paid a fair bit of attention to all the matches, whether they were challenge games or league or championship. No matter what game I played, I would go to win it and even if it was tiddly-winks… you wanted to win it.

We were training at least two times a week.

James Tiernan was the trainer, who was deeply involved in soccer in Sligo and he did the training with us… it was fairly good training, I have to say, it was lively and he'd get you fit. You'd have a fair bit of ball work as well but then again, we were probably lucky with that 1975 team, there was a good few of the minors from '68 that came through.

The injection of youth definitely helped things.

They had competed at a high level – to beat Armagh in an All-Ireland semi-final in 1968, and then to go on and to be beaten by a point by Cork, they had great experience, those lads… John Brennan and those lads. They were the backbone of the team.

I was marking Tommy Joe Gilmore the day of the semi-final, he was centre-back for Galway. I would have a great memory of laying off some good ball into Mickey Kearins inside in full-forward, and he did a fair bit of scoring that day.

I'd probably add a point or two for the game that time, but you'd be passing it around too.

I think we surprised Galway on the day.

We gave them a good beating. They weren't able to stay with us. I'd say they were just down to play us and that was it, they got caught on the hop. Probably some people on that team were gone past it, but the fact we had so many of the minors from 1968 in the team was huge. I don't think anyone dwelled on that, but they were brilliant. Even in training that win gave us a lot of confidence. Training was very lively after that.

I don't remember a lot about the first match in the Connacht final – they hit the crossbar and that meant it ended up as a draw. I don't think we were lucky to get the draw that day, if anything we probably threw it away.

But that was the norm for Sligo teams… it was always that point or two points. We were glad to get another chance at it.

To beat Mayo in Castlebar in a replay was no mean feat.

I was thinking back on 1975 and the preparation for those games, and the preparation for games today are just miles and miles apart. I travelled to that game with two couples in a car the whole way to Castlebar.

There was no such thing as a bus. A good mate of mine, Paddy Hargadon (RIP) picked me up at the gate and brought me to the game… and he brought me home again after. At that time too, sometimes you'd be hitching into and home from training.

I think we might have gone direct to the pitch. We did have a meal in the Breaffy House afterwards. I'd have a fair recollection of the match.

It was a tense battle, but a lot of the time when you get out on the field the whole thing changes; there's no nerves, there's no talk anymore. You go hell for leather at it. I remember distinctly now. It's amazing how time moves on – just a year ago there was a bit on YouTube of the game and I was kicking a point!

I remember Des Kearins getting the goal towards the end… that was a big score. I scored four points. I was fairly happy with the performance.

It was a huge thing for the area, even to represent the club and all that. It was a nice honour for me to be on the team, being from north Sligo.

I can remember the feeling well at the final whistle, because I had family home from England who were in the crowd and I knew where they were, so I went over to them. It was just a fantastic feeling. There was joy everywhere… it was 1928 since we had won it before. It was amazing.

It had a big impact on the supporters too.

I was in the ESB and I was very friendly with a fella in town, and I used to stay with him the odd time. He was telling me he had a younger brother and they were out playing football in the green… pretending to be the Sligo players.

It was amazing how the young people picked up on it. That's nearly the most important part of successes – that's what it's all about.

We were back into training again soon enough after because Kerry were on the horizon at that stage.

There was a lot of excitement heading up to Croke Park.

For a start we weren't too far off Kerry, but they pulled away. We only scored five points that day. It was a nice honour to play in Croke Park again for me, because I played there with an under-16 vocational schools hurling team and then I played there as well with Dundalk Regional College in 1973.

1975 is one of the big memories I have. I also scored 3-8 against London, that would be a big thing too. That was just about being in the right place at the right time, that's half the battle. And of course, London wouldn't be a highly rated team either.

I definitely could have scored more too but I took the foot off the pedal in the last 15 minutes.

I played up to 1982 and I enjoyed the football. It's nice to have been part of the team that got the Connacht title.

I have daughters who played for Drumcliffe/Rosses Point and won a Connacht junior medal. So mine is not the only Connacht medal in the house.

I have to thank my wife Pat and family for all the times I was missing out of the house.

But I must say we got great enjoyment out of the GAA.

BARNES MURPHY

Captain, trainer and coach... Barnes Murphy completed the work of two or three men through the glorious summer of 1975.

66

IN THE EARLY years, there was no tradition of gaelic football in our area and, furthermore, as children we were not permitted to play football at our local school, Stokane national school. The school was located two miles from my home place, which was halfway between the Ox Mountains and Enniscrone, close to the Mayo border.

From the age of five or six I was obsessed with playing football and when we didn't own a real ball, we sometimes made one from wet newspapers or some other material. Eventually our cousin Fr Christopher McLoughlin, a student in Rome in the 50s, bought a new leather football for us.

A field beside our house was the place of choice for all the neighbours and us to amuse ourselves; there were Gallaghers, Igoes, Cawleys, Brennans and Foodys, as well as other youngsters on their way to the bog to save the turf. My father would regularly keep an eye on us, especially as there was always the possibility our kitchen window would be accidentally broken by someone! In time, my passion led to the organizing of a team to play at Dromore West sports day. We all cycled the 10-mile journey to and from the game.

In 1962 I was sent to boarding school at St Nathy's College, Ballaghaderreen. From the perspective of football, I won juvenile and junior Connacht medals, although our team was defeated in a number of senior finals. In St Nathy's we had Mayo, Roscommon and Sligo minor players, including the late great Dermot Earley, who played for Roscommon and was one of the most likeable, humble and gentlemanly players I ever had the privilege to meet.

Growing up I tended to associate with Mayo football having read the *Western People* about their great teams of the 50s.

In 1963 and '64, I played minor football with the Bonniconlon club in Mayo. A neighbour, Jimmy Foody would call to our home to ask me to play – it was an opportunity to get away from the drudgery of farm work! As well as that, Sergeant Joe McManus from Enniscrone – a true Gaelgeoir – attended the St Nathy's games and consequently invited me to play minor for Enniscrone. That year, in 1965, we were supposedly beaten by a point in the county final, but, due to an error by the referee Enniscrone were also awarded medals.

We won the county junior final the following year.

On one particular occasion on my way to play a match in Enniscrone, I met with Willie and Oliver Fox, who convinced me the match in Enniscrone was called off; they persuaded me to travel with them to play for Bonninconlon against Kiltane in Bangor Erris. Later, I met with a disgruntled Sergeant McManus, who enquired as to why I didn't turn up for Enniscrone on the same day.

I advised him that I was informed the match was cancelled but I did not tell him about the escapade of going to Bangor Erris to play Kiltane! As we were late reaching Erris, we missed the photo-shoot for the *Western People* and so I was saved the embarrassment. The Fox brothers often reminded me of the trick they played, and how I fell for it!

I continued to play under-21 football for Sligo in 1966, '67 and '68, and a senior challenge game in '67 allowed me the opportunity to play at right half-back against the famous Joe Corcoran, a Mayo legend. Snow fell on the pitch and the game was called off.

Alongside Sean Davey at midfield on the Sligo league team of 1968, I was taken off in the second-half and put back on against Cavan's Ray Carolan – we won, but lost in a replay of the league semi-final the same year against a great Kildare team.

My father and our neighbour Pat Igoe were stalwart supporters.

When listening to Sligo games on the radio my father would often leave the kitchen and take a walk, as sometimes the tension and excitement became too much. Whenever I met with Pat all he ever wanted to know was, 'What kind of a fella is Mickey Kearins?' and... 'Would he ever talk to you?'

As the records show, Mickey was Sligo's greatest ever gaelic footballer, who had a lion's heart, and could kick points from all angles; although he never won an All-Ireland medal he richly deserved to be included into the GAA Hall of Fame.

In the lead up to 1975, we had some narrow misses in the championship.

When the ban on foreign games was lifted in 1971, Sligo was lucky to get hold of two magnificent players in David Pugh and Gerry Mitchell, who played a significant role in us winning against Roscommon in the first round of the championship, and in the Connacht final when we lost to Galway. I received a leg injury in the drawn game... I wasn't ready for the replay.

In 1972, I played at centre-back for Sligo against Mayo in Markievicz Park... we drew. Mayo won the replay by a point or two in extra-time at Castlebar – they had super players like John Morley, Joe Corcoran, Joe Langan, Ray Prendergast and the brilliant Johnny Carey.

The following year we reached the league semi-final against Offaly in Croke Park. Offaly won the 1971 and '72 All Ireland finals. I marked Kevin Kilmurray in the final of the Railway Cup – a draw – a few days before the league semi-final.

Mickey Kearins scored 13 or 14 points in the Railway Cup game... he couldn't miss! Unfortunately, we lost to Offaly in that semi-final.

We lost to Roscommon in both the league semi-final and the Connacht Championship in 1974 – both games were replays. On the four occasions I marked

Dermot Earley, who moved to centrefield during the second-half in both replays… I often regretted not following him out to the middle. I was selected for an All Star that year at centre-back and Dermot was awarded an All Star at midfield.

Winning such an award at that time was incredible, with a trip to San Francisco, Los Angeles and New York over three whole weeks. The All Star team was managed by the great Sean Purcell of Galway, who was considered to be one of the best all-round footballers that ever played. He was a truly genuine character… I had the pleasure to meet him in Tuam on a couple of occasions.

The Dublin All Stars were tough on the field but perfect gentlemen without the ball in their hands. Their manager Kevin Heffernan was a wonderful mentor and great for advice when I needed it, especially when Sligo played Galway that year.

On route to New York, meeting with Willie Joyce at Shannon was a little awkward at first since we had some hard battles over the years – however, many of that group became good friends… John Hughes, Tommy Naughton and John Tobin.

On one occasion, Willie made reference to playing Sligo in the first round of the championship.

'Sure, ye will play well for 50 minutes… but we will win in the last 10 minutes!' he told me.

I was captain, trainer and coach that year.

I used Willie's exclamation at every training session!

We played Galway a few weeks later in the Connacht semi-final and won by 10 points. Afterwards I was glad to meet Willie and tell him, 'We played for the full 60 minutes today!'

In the final we had a lucky draw with Mayo on home soil when in the last minute JP Kean cracked the ball off the crossbar after a great run and pass from Tommy O'Malley.

Against all the odds, we defeated Mayo in the replay at Castlebar to win the first Connacht final for the county in 48 years. It was a magnificent feat following so many tough losses over several years.

The All-Ireland semi-final was a different story.

Prior to that game, I invited Brian McEniff from Donegal to come along to our training sessions, and I also asked both Brian and John 'Tull' Dunne of

Galway to come to Croke Park to give a team talk before the big game.

Both men obliged, although they didn't appear at half-time.

Later, I discovered Brian and John were snubbed by the Sligo selectors when they suggested some changes during the first-half. At the time, it seemed there was a lack of belief and trust in their advice when it could have made a difference.

In my opinion, Sligo failed to build on the success of 1975.

I played my club football with Craobh Rua from 1972… they later amalgamated with Mhuire Naofa to form St Mary's GAA Club. The club won county finals in 1977, '79, '80 and '81, and Connacht titles in 1977, '79 and '81. In 1977, we played Thomond College of Limerick, who had all county players on their side.

Thomond won by a slim four points. It was a golden decade for club football in Sligo, especially since no Sligo town team had won the Senior Championship since 1954.

In 1972, the Sligo team manager James Nicholson had invited me to play for Sligo in New York. It was their first time to win the championship, and I travelled to New York on several occasions.

One particular time in Gaelic Park, as we entered we noticed the spectators were completely silent… and when we enquired as to what was happening someone uttered, 'SSSHHHHHHH… Mick O'Connell is playing!'

When the game was over the crowd assembled in John Kerry O'Donnell's pub when, lo and behold, O'Connell entered and once again silence descended on the patrons. Mick duly walked to our table, shook my hand and welcomed me to New York, as well as enquiring about the well-being of Mickey Kearins.

O'Connell was the undisputed maestro of gaelic football over the decades; he was a kind of enigma who intrigued players and supporters. Meeting him was a great privilege and a proud moment for me.

Looking back at the 60s, the Down team changed the style of football with the short kick passing between players… it served them well as they won All-Irelands in 1960 and '61. The great three in-a-row Galway team carried on the trend with talented players such as 18-year-old Jimmy Duggan coming in at midfield in 1966. The Dublin and Kerry teams of the 70s and 80s were equally as good.

However, I believe goal scoring with the hand spoiled those games.

It was great to see Donegal win an All-Ireland in 1992 with Brian McEniff as manager, and again in 2012 with Jim McGuinness at the helm – having the assistance of the brilliant Michael Murphy… one of the best footballers in Ireland.

I found the victorious Derry team of 1993 winning the All-Ireland with the notable Eamon Coleman as manager a unique occasion too.

I cannot forget ex-St Nathy's man John O'Mahony, who managed Leitrim to a Connacht final in 1994, and took his native Mayo so close to an of All Ireland title before finally managing Galway to win two All-Irelands in 1998 and 2001.

Finally, over the years it was great to share some highs and lows of gaelic football with wonderful colleagues and friends.

I think it was Mick O'Connell who said, 'I never treated a win on the football field as a triumph… nor a defeat as a disaster'.

I am not certain I could share the same sentiments as Mick!

MICK LAFFEY
(& JOHN KENT)

SLIGO 2-9 ROSCOMMON 1-8
Connacht SFC Semi-Final
Markievicz Park
JUNE 14 1981

Defeating Roscommon to return to the Connacht final of 1981 is a memory Mick Laffey (front row with the ball at his feet) holds closer to his heart than winning the provincial final in 1975.

★ **SLIGO:** J Murphy; C Murphy, D Foley, F Finan; M Brennan, **M Laffey**, P Henry; M McCarrick, J Stenson (0-1); J Kearins (2-1), S Durkin, **J Kent (0-3)**; M Hoey (0-3), PJ Kavanagh (0-1), E McHale. Subs: L Wynne for Hoey, B Murphy for Brennan.

★ **ROSCOMMON:** G Sheerin; H Keegan, P Lindsay, J McManus; P Fitzmaurice, T Donlon, G Connellan; D Earley (1-3), G Beirne; A Dooley, L Dolphin (0-2), J O'Gara; M Finneran, T McManus (0-1), G Emmett. Subs: J Connellan for Fitzmaurice, J O'Connor for Emmett.

THE ACTION

A ROSCOMMON SIDE expected to swat aside the challenge of Sligo with considerable ease got a rude awakening at Markievicz Park as the home team romped home to a deserved win.

In what was the county's best result in the province since winning the title in 1975, Sligo displayed grit and determination to inflict a first defeat in Connacht on Roscommon in five seasons.

Barnes Murphy's men led from start to finish, with James Kearins firing in the all-important goals.

Mattie Hoey, who was withdrawn through injury, and John Kent also contributed handsomely to the winner's cause, kicking three points apiece, while PJ Kavanagh, Martin McCarrick and Francie Finan were among the others to catch the eye in black and white. Mick Laffey, in the unusual position of centre-back, was also a steadying influence in a Sligo defence that thwarted Roscommon's efforts on numerous occasions.

It was a timely lift for the county, who had seen their fortunes decline since they scaled the summit some six years previously. Apart from a win over London in 1978, Sligo had no championship successes under their belt in that period.

Roscommon, with eyes on a prize beyond Connacht perhaps having contested, and very nearly won, the previous year's All-Ireland final, never led in an encounter which was dominated by Sligo – 0-6 to 0-3 up at half-time, the Yeats County pressed home their superiority in the second period with Kearins on target for two goals to help Sligo into a 2-7 to 0-4 lead.

Although Dermot Earley's late goal threatened Sligo's lead, the home side were not to be denied as they held out for a deserved victory and a place in the Connacht final against Mayo.

★ ★ ★ ★ ★

"

THERE'S NOT REALLY one game that stands out for me, there's bits of different games. With all the years with Sligo, I've only ever played in two Connacht finals... 1975 and the other in '81.

But, Roscommon played in the All-Ireland final in 1980 and we drew them in the first round of the championship the following year. That was special. It was the first time I played at centre-back.

John Kent got three points and James Kearins got two goals. Barnes Murphy was in charge of the team.

Afterwards, going into the Connacht final against Mayo, I felt that we were in with a great chance because we played reasonably well against Roscommon, but we fell flat... we only scored four points.

For me growing up, I really wanted to play for Sligo in the big games.

In the 60s, when I was 12 to 14 years of age, my father was chairman of the County Board and he brought me to matches all over the place. I grew up with that. My dad played with Mayo, and won an All-Ireland in 1936, so I think it was in the genes... or in the blood.

When he was chairman, he was involved with the team selection as well, and going to matches they used to gather at our house in the morning before they got into a few cars and headed away to matches. So, I was brought up with that... that was the big thing for me, I just wanted to play.

I was at a match between Sligo and Galway, and Mickey Durkin from Tourlestrane was playing full-forward and scored two goals in the first-half. Galway went on to win the All-Ireland after that. They got a grip on the game and pipped it at the end... that was in the mid-60s.

I played my underage football with a team called Muire Naofa, which is now St Mary's.

My Dad didn't really have too much to say about my football, even though he knew all about it and was a successful player himself. He encouraged me to play but it was really up to myself. He came to the games, but he would never say after a game that I should have done this... or I should have done that.

I played minor football for Sligo and was in the squad in 1969 and '70. The 1968 minor team… most of them had moved on by then, although I think Des Kearins was still underage the following year. We got beaten early in the championship.

I loved it, all I wanted to do was play, much to the dissatisfaction of my mother I think… I wasn't doing much homework! But so be it.

I came into the senior squad probably around 1973.

Mickey Kearins was in charge and he brought myself and a few more in; Johnny Stenson also came on the scene around that time. I would have been getting 15 or 20 minutes in a league game or a challenge game at the time, and in 1973 I came on at half-time against Galway in the championship in Tuam. A frightening experience to be landed into.

I was scared… I was so nervous!

A lot of the game that time was catch and kick… catch and deliver. It was all about delivering the ball first time and getting it up the field as quickly as possible.

I was there in 1975 when we won the Connacht Championship, but I suppose a lot of it went over my head. I wasn't playing that long and I was lucky. The aftermath of 1975 was the big thing… we were in every half-parish in the county.

The 1971 team was a much better team; they were unlucky and if they had won something they might have presented Sligo as a stronger force to go forward. After 1975, a good few left and retired. It was probably a little bit more difficult to progress after that.

When St Mary's was set up in 1976, we enjoyed some good success at club level for a number of years.

The difference I make between club and county is… playing with St Mary's we won the championship in 1977 and played in Connacht and won that, and then we're going on to play in an All-Ireland semi-final. With the club, it was always drilled into us that we were good enough… good enough… good enough!

Being beaten by Thomond College by four points was no bad result, even though we were really disappointed. We had a real belief.

I don't know if that full belief was there with Sligo. Had we been bombarded with that sort of belief going into the All-Ireland semi-final in 1975 would it have made any difference? Maybe… maybe not, it's very hard to tell at this stage.

It was brilliant to be involved with St Mary's success, and the thing was, you were playing football all year round. The National League that time started in October, and if you were playing with Sligo in the championship we were one game... or two games and we might be gone. But then we were straight back into the club scene which was great. We just loved playing so regularly and for so long, and one game just went into the next. There was no real break or downtime.

The club stuff did give us confidence going into Sligo. We were used to success and we believed we could win.

There was no backdoor... it all rested on one game.

If you got a chance again the following week, who knows what might have happened, but Sligo could have had a better championship record.

Prior to 1981 I was playing in the forward line, but Barnes put me back to centre-back that year. I actually enjoyed playing there as it turned out, it was a new place for me... I think I might have played a game or two at midfield as well before that but, generally, I was always in the forwards. It's like everything else, I'd say Barnes probably took a chance putting me back there to try it out and see if it'd work.

It obviously did a bit because I played there for a while after!

The approach for that Roscommon match was the same as going into any game. You go in having prepared well, you believe you can win, you put the same amount of training in as any of the other teams around the place. Whether we had the real confidence we should have had going in, or whether we were able to display confidence and that strong belief that we were going out here and could win this... it's hard to know.

I can only say how I felt and I certainly believed we could do it, and I think everyone else was of the same mindset. You needed 25 lads to be thinking the same way to be successful and I'm sure we did.

We would be training the same as everyone else, plenty of running and plenty of ball; the emphasis was probably more on running than ball skills in the early days. As the games developed and as we developed, there was more ball, more ball skills and more ball training came into play.

Training-wise, when I started my banking career I was working in Tuam and in 1975 we played Galway in the championship... but I was training with Galway in 1974. So I started to travel to Sligo for training and once I started doing that

I never missed a night… two nights a week travelling down to Sligo from Tuam. Frank Henry usually travelled with me too.

The roads were cat, and the cars weren't great but you didn't think about it, you just did it and I felt I was part of something good and I was enjoying it, and felt fortunate to be playing in it.

It was good to train with Galway. They were very good to me, they welcomed me in and they allowed me to do everything that they were doing and there was never any of them pushing me away to do other things. I was always part of the group and that was it.

I was only in with them for a couple of months in Tuam when they were training for championship and that sort of stuff.

If you think of the early part of my career, in the 70s and into the early-80s, we didn't have a lot of money to go anywhere, so we spent a lot of our time and evenings up in Markievicz Park or some pitch kicking ball. There might have been two, three or five of us, whoever was available would go up and you might spend two or three hours – we spent a lot of evenings up there kicking, shooting points, soloing, doing some tackling and all of that sort of stuff.

Roscommon had the game nearly won against Kerry in the All-Ireland final of 1980. They were playing into the elements in the second-half and their half-forwards maybe came a little too deep and they found it very difficult to dig the ball out past the halfway line, because they had really driven the game in the early part of it.

They were really flying and we all thought they were going to win the game but it ended up that they couldn't dig it out because of playing into the wind.

Looking at the game in 1981 from centre half-back that day, we had Martin McCarrick and Johnny Stenson at midfield so they would have been quite strong; we would have been hoping they would break even at least at midfield and keep the ball going forward and it'd be up to us to close down their forward line as best we could.

Paddy Henry and Mattie Brennan were either side of me, two brilliant guys. They made my job easier and because they were so good, they allowed me to go forward from time to time as well.

I can't really remember much of the game but we probably shell-shocked them and as we got a grip on the game, they just weren't able to get back into it; sometimes a game like that drifts away from you and the harder you try the worse it gets. The way I remember it, we got the edge on them and I don't know what got into them. You don't know how their preparations went but ours went very well.

When you're playing a team that has been beaten in the All-Ireland final, or a team at that level, you go in really charged to try and beat them, saying that we're pitching ourselves against the best.

Then, once we got over that it gave the county a great lift and we were in with a great chance. We were playing Mayo... down to Castlebar and I thought we were in with a good shout but four points tells you a lot about the day.

We kicked a bagful of wides... a lot of wides.

We had enough possession to be a lot closer to them but we had a lot of wides, which is very frustrating and we were all just so disappointed coming away from a result like that. When you believed that you were in with a great chance of winning, to come out and lose like that on a scoreline of 0-12 to 0-4, kicking a lot of chances away and not being at your best. It's hard.

I'm fortunate that I can look back on an enjoyable career with Sligo.

So, to have that... gives me great satisfaction.

JOHN KENT

John Kent (left of photo, with Thomas Jordan in the 2008 Connacht Championship) believes Sligo could have achieved so much more in the 80s.

"

IN 1976 I went on a soccer scholarship to America.

I played a lot of football that year as well. St Mary's was formed in 1976 and I played that first year when we got to the county final. I left for America the week before the final and I remember the chairman of the club phoned me.

I had arrived in the U.S. on a Wednesday, and the following Wednesday he phoned me to see if I would come back to play the final on the Sunday!

I couldn't do it.

In my second game out there I got a bad injury. I tore my medial ligament off the bone... I still have a staple in my knee from it. I was supposed to wear a big hinge knee support. I was on a four-year scholarship, but I came back in the summer and played with St Mary's and that was the year we won our first Sligo title.

I was supposed to go back to college in August. I said to the coach, 'Look… we've the final this week… I'll play this and then I'll go back'. We were playing St Pat's. We didn't know if we'd win or not, but we did and went on into Connacht, so I didn't go back to America. I stayed and played the season with St Mary's.

Sligo Rovers wanted me to sign that year as well but I was committed to the gaelic. We got beaten in the All-Ireland semi-final by Thomond College… they had the Spillanes, Talty… a lot of county players playing.

I had played soccer for a season with Sligo Rovers in 1973/74, and then I went on trial to Celtic in the summer of 1975.

I actually didn't go to the replay of the Connacht final in Castlebar the day before because I was joining up with Celtic on the Monday; they were coming over to Ireland on tour, and I was afraid I'd be tired. I was at the game in Sligo but not in Castlebar.

I was with Celtic for three or four weeks. They played a few games against Dundalk, Finn Harps and Sligo Rovers. I came on as a token sub against Rovers but it was fantastic. Kenny Dalglish and all these guys were there.

I tell people that Celtic kept Kenny Dalglish and let me go!

With Summerhill in 1975 we won the Connacht schools 'A' title in gaelic football. One regret I have is that we should have won the All-Ireland semi-final; we threw away that game against St Colman's from Newry; we should have got to the All-Ireland final. I did my Leaving Cert in 1975, and in '76 I was capped for the Irish Youths six or seven times, and played with Sligo Rovers as well that year.

I probably could have played soccer professionaly, and I did enjoy it. People say to me that my father was a founding member of St Mary's and that he didn't want me to play soccer, but that couldn't be further from the truth. I didn't realise at the time, but he used to go to all the games as well. When I came back from America and because of my knee injury, I found with soccer that there is more contact with your lower body than in gaelic football, which is more upper body. When I came back to Ireland I discarded the knee brace… I played without it, and St Mary's went on the run. Had we been beaten I probably would've turned back to soccer because I wasn't doing anything for the winter, so it was just the way it went.

And because of the club set-up I was friendly with the lads in the football and we had a social life afterwards too. It was harder to break that cycle then. I played a bit of junior soccer when there was no gaelic on over the following years.

To win with your own club was great.

As I've said, my father was one of the founding members of the club, and my brother Jim was playing as well... it was a great time. All the guys we played with were our friends. Even my parents used to come out on a Sunday night after the game; that's when we had a few drinks and a bit of fun. There was a huge pride in that, in winning. St Mary's were formed in 1976 – Craobh Rua had been the senior team in town up to that and Muire Naofa were the underage team. A lot of the guys with Craobh Rua were trying to win a senior championship but never got there, and then the first year of St Mary's we ended up getting to a county final and won the next one.

They got the success they deserved having been knocking on the door; they would have come up against St Pat's and Mickey Kearins for a number of years. Back then people were delighted to see a new town team come along and in 1978 against St Pat's people were actually up for us that time, which is hard to believe now!

The first time I was selected for Sligo at senior level was for the opening of the pitch in Grange, but it was called off because of some storm. The first championship game I played for the county was when I came back for the summer in 1977 and was brought into the panel straight away. Sligo played Roscommon in Hyde Park. I was only a sub, but I came on and was taking a free from 25 yards out, going for a point and I completely mishit it, but it went into Johnny Stenson's arms and he turned and scored a goal... and people thought it was a great pass!

Brendan McCauley was the manager and then Barnes came in and was in charge in 1981 when we beat Roscommon. I always felt as a county we should have put more emphasis on the league. Back in the 60s Sligo were a Division One team, and there or thereabouts, but things slipped. Most of the football I played was in Division Four because we were struggling – maybe the thought was... *We'll concentrate on the championship...* but really you have to be playing a higher level in the league to get a couple of good wins in the summer.

That win over Roscommon was probably the highlight of my career with Sligo, but then we got beaten in the final – I was terrible, I missed a load of frees. And you think… *Well, we'll be back next year…* but I never played in a Connacht final again after. That's the way it goes.

When I was in Summerhill, I was a good free-taker, but I lost that and I didn't practice enough maybe. I was always fit. In America I was put on weight training to help my knee – which was unheard of here at the time – and I kept that going when I came home. I was very conscious I needed to keep my legs strong. But I didn't go out and practice frees as I should have.

The first thing that happened in games at that time was that the back would thump or kick the forward… that's what you got! And you could look at a linesman or an umpire but they didn't want to know about it. There was a lot of pulling and dragging too, a lot of that went on. That's why I'd love to play now because that's gone out of the game, thankfully, which is good.

When I was starting to play with St Mary's we'd go to a lot of tournaments in north Mayo and west Sligo – we'd often play a league match in the afternoon and then maybe go and play a tournament match in Easkey or somewhere. Sure all the games would end up in fights and brawls.

And then afterwards you'd go and have a few pints and everyone was friends then again…mad stuff altogether!

As my father would say… 'We got more muck than memories', but we had great fun, far more fun than there is now. Brilliant memories.

Another standout game for me was the first time I played Railway Cup. It was in the early-80s and I played centre-forward for Connacht that day, with Dermot Earley and Brian Talty and Barry Brennan. I really liked centre-forward… most of the time I played with Sligo I was left half-forward. I liked centre-forward more because you were able to get more involved, but Sligo never really played me there because they probably felt they needed someone bigger and stronger.

I remember somebody cried off the morning of the game. Tom Heneghan from Roscommon was managing the team and he brought a new level of professionalism to the training – we had trained the morning of the match, and whoever was playing centre-forward dropped out. He told me I was going in there and just told me to play my own game.

As I say, I was probably coming from a low base and with not much confidence that I could play at that level the first few times, but I played well that day. I enjoyed it. I linked in with guys and held my place. It was another big disappointment then when we lost to Munster in the final in Cusack Park in Ennis. The next year, I scored a goal in the last few minutes against Munster in Tullamore but it was disallowed for a square ball. We could have won it, against all those lads from the great Kerry team. It would have meant so much to us.

I took a lot from playing with those players. I loved training but compared to now there's such a difference with training... with science and diets. A lot of lads in my era were definitely dehydrated when we played because there was little knowledge of hydration, or even diet. I remember when we'd be playing a championship match in Markievicz Park, we might meet up in the Sligo Park Hotel at two o'clock for tea and ham sandwiches. Most teams were the same. I enjoyed the intensity of the training with Connacht.

Tom Heneghan was manager of Roscommon when they got to the All-Ireland final in 1980 and you could see what they were doing; there was an intensity that maybe we lacked here. Everything was done with the ball... all game-based drills. I loved it and should have learned something from it.

Speaking personally, when I was playing with Connacht in those years I felt that I was as good as any of the players playing. Without being cocky, I felt we could compete with Roscommon and the other teams in Connacht but, as regards winning, I wouldn't say we really expected to beat Roscommon. We went out with more hope than confidence. They were looking at winning an All-Ireland – a trip down to Sligo was going to be tricky but everyone thought they were going to win it.

Because of my involvement with Connacht I knew a lot of the lads. I knew John O'Gara going back to Summerhill College, Tony McManus, Seamus Hayden, Dermot Earley... they were all really nice lads and when I was playing with Connacht they really instilled belief in me and gave me confidence that I could play at that level. While they were gutted and shocked at getting beaten, I had a few drinks with them after the game – they were obviously very disappointed to lose but they wished us well. We wouldn't have shown any great form coming up to the match.

Whereas Roscommon were probably looking beyond Connacht at a bigger prize. I know from talking to Tom Heneghan – he was the manager still – that he was worried coming to Sligo but really people didn't think that we could do it.

It wasn't that we trained particularly hard before that but it was one of those days where we clicked and we got confident on the day, and that got us across the line. I remember taking a ball… Harry Keegan was coming out of defence and I went to challenge him as he soloed the ball and it went up in the air. I grabbed it out of his hand, turned around and fed it inside and we actually got a penalty out of that move. Mick Laffey scored the goal. It was a big score in the game.

We qualified for the Connacht final and maybe, as we always do in Sligo, people got a bit carried away – and I missed so many chances that day.

I think Mattie Hoey got injured before the game so I was taking the frees and I had a nightmare that day. But I had one great chance. Late on in the game I came onto a ball that broke inside and I should have scored a goal. I just hit it too hard and it went over the bar. It was one of those days. We were relatively young and wouldn't have had a huge amount of experience, but it was a bad day out.

We'd Martin McCarrick, Johnny Stenson was still there, Mick Laffey played centre-back that year having converted from wing forward to the backs… Anthony Brennan was playing. We'd good players but we were coming from a low base and we didn't have the confidence in ourselves that maybe we should have had.

We were languishing down in Division Three and Four, maybe not preparing as well as we could have. It was a different era and we didn't do an awful lot of training in the winter, which I always thought was a mistake – we should have concentrated on getting up a few divisions. We weren't going to turn up and win a championship out of nowhere. And then the draw at that time kept Mayo and Galway apart, so they couldn't meet until the final. We had to beat the two of them to win a Connacht title, so the draw was unfair to us too. I just think we didn't have enough belief… that's just the way it was.

We would talk about winning the Connacht Championship. We'd be looking at the draw and thinking we had what it took to win it. Was it realistic? Maybe not.

But I think we could have done a lot better… we underachieved and underperformed. But that Roscommon win was a big one for us at the time.

99

FINTAN FEENEY

SLIGO 0-12 LONDON 0-9
Connacht SFC Quarter-Final
Ruislip
JUNE 6 1993

Sligo needed Fintan Feeney to be at his very best from play and placed balls, in order to avoid a humiliating defeat to London in Ruislip in 1993.

★ **SLIGO:** P Kilcoyne; B Deignan, D Keaveney, B Kilcoyne (0-1); B Tuohy, T Breheny, B Mulhern (0-1); S Tully, P Durcan; T Deignan (0-1), PJ Barrins, P Seevers; K Barrins, **F Feeney (0-8)**, E Molloy. Subs: D Hannon (0-1) for Barrins, K Kearins for Molloy.

★ **LONDON:** G Boyle; M Somers, J McCormack, P Guinan; G Feeron (0-1), F O'Dowd, P Cullen; M Heslin, J Costello; L Molloy, E Prenten (0-4), T Maguire (0-2); J Landy (0-2), T McBride, R Henneberry. Subs: M McLoughlin for Costello, N Harrington for Henneberry, T Gallagher for Guinan.

THE ACTION

WITH FIVE MINUTES to go in Ruislip, Sligo were staring down the barrel of an historic defeat.

London, who hadn't won in the province since 1977 when they beat Leitrim, had the visitors in trouble in front of 2,000 spectators in north west London, but eventually Sligo turned the screw late on to progress to a Connacht semi-final with Mayo.

After a difficult decade through the 80s, the 90s had started in a similar fashion for a county in a transitional phase, though a close game with Mayo the previous summer suggested Sligo could be a coming force once again.

However, in the English capital it was a case of being lucky to escape with their ambitions intact, with London providing significant resistance all the way through.

Sligo were thankful for the services of full-forward Fintan Feeney, with the Easkey man kicking eight points in all. Some of these, coming in the closing stages, saw Sligo edge in front after London had held the ascendency.

Still, the visitors had some promising spells. They dominated the midfield area, where Shane Tully and Paul Durcan enjoyed a productive hour, while Brendan Kilcoyne and Bernard Mulhern also raided forward from defence to raise white flags.

London enjoyed a lot of possession at various stages but were quite wasteful up front. Still, they held the lead heading into the final five minutes by a single point. Sligo summoned a strong finish, coupled with Feeney's accuracy, to avoid a major banana skin and emerge with their credentials just about intact.

But Sligo's Robbie Henneberry and Francis O'Dowd were among the London forwards.

★★★★★

"

GROWING UP AS a young lad in Easkey, football meant everything to me. Every evening I was out in the nearest field kicking the ball around with neighbours.

Playing in Killeenduff national school was the start of it all. I went on to play with Easkey at club level starting with the under-12s. We won several West Division titles up to minor level, eventually winning the county minor championship in 1980 when we beat St Mary's

I went to Sligo games as a youngster, with my dad, in across the hill in Markievicz to watch matches. That was the mid-70s when Padraic Calpin and Robert Connolly from Easkey were part of the team. One game in particular that still stands out for me was Sligo playing Roscommon… Dermot Earley scored a fantastic goal from about 30 yards.

As a family we went to a lot of Easkey matches too. The local tournaments were the big thing in those days, in Culleens and in Easkey. I played in a few of the tournaments in my mid-teens. It was usually hard football, no referees were really needed!

Everyone got involved… the lads on the line… everyone! It was wild when you look back on it!

I remember Mickey Kearins well growing up.

I used to hear so much about him. He was a brilliant footballer. I watched him playing local tournament games and the odd county game. He was coming to the end of his career at that time but he was still a marked man.

However, it never really crossed my mind about playing for Sligo when I was growing up, though I was on the county minor panel for a while.

After Easkey won the Intermediate Championship in 1982 I was asked by the Shannon Blues club to play with them in Boston – I travelled over with my cousin Brendan Feeney. The Shannon Blues had strong Sligo connections.

I played for them in Boston in 1983 and in '84 and, on occasion, would travel to New York to play with the Mayo team in Gaelic Park. The standard of football was very high at that time due to the amount of inter-county players that came over from Ireland for the summer.

When I came home in 1985 the recession had hit Ireland badly and a lot of my former Easkey teammates had emigrated to different parts of the world.

Easkey were struggling with numbers and as a result had dropped down to intermediate level. We managed to win the championship again in 1987 with younger lads coming through. At that time we had a mix of young and older lads, with some exceptional players.

My own fitness levels after America were good so I didn't find county training too hard. Not only was I doing hard physical work over there but the club had Bruno Byrne, a former Dublin under-21 player training us. The training was tough, especially in 80 degrees heat.

Our ball work and tactics were all about quick thinking… quick hands and quick feet!

I was picked on the county panel for the first time in 1985 based on my performance for the club. I didn't mind where we went or who we were playing, I just loved playing football. I was competitive and I gave one hundred percent every time I played – I wanted to win. But win or lose, I enjoyed it.

When you enjoy something you will always do your best.

I played with the county team over the years in every forward position, but mainly wing forward. My first championship game for Sligo was in 1986… corner-forward against Galway in Markievicz Park. Galway beat us that day.

No matter who we met in the Connacht Championship, it was always going to be a tough challenge but we always gave it our best. Looking back, we probably gave those teams too much respect and maybe didn't believe in ourselves enough.

We'd a couple of good performances before 1993, coming close enough but at the same time just never good enough to get across the line. There were good Mayo teams at that time – they were coming through from Connacht, and they weren't getting hammered when they left Connacht either.

In 1993, we travelled to Ruislip to play London in the championship.

We didn't know much about London at the time, only that the year before they ran Mayo close enough and that two former Sligo players were on the team – Francis Dowd and Robbie Henneberry, both good players.

It was a particularly warm day in London.

We started off well but we didn't get the scores. It was tit-for-tat most of the way. Everyone was a bit nervous because London were the whipping boys in Connacht at that time. They hadn't won a championship since they beat Leitrim in 1977 but everyone knew they were getting better.

We were nervous; there was an expectation and we didn't want to be the next team to get beaten by London. I was full-forward but switched out in the second-half when we were two points down and coming under a bit of pressure

I went out centerfield after a while. I didn't win clean possession out there, but I won a few breaking balls. In the past I had played one or two games in the middle for Sligo but most of my playing career was in the forwards... full-forward was my favourite position.

I got a goal chance early in the game. I won a ball in the corner, got around my man but when I got inside him, I only managed to hit the side netting.

They were sticking close to us all the way through... with minutes to go it was anyone's game. They went a point ahead. It was tense.

We were all feeling the pressure.

With five minutes to go our luck changed. We got on top and scored four points in the last few minutes of the game.

For me, I always went out as just a player on the team. I wanted to play all the time and loved playing, but when you're a forward you're probably a bit more in the spotlight than the backs.

I wasn't always kicking the frees for Sligo in those years. I did for a while under different managers and had good days and bad days. After scoring eight points in London, I missed a couple of frees in the semi-final in Markievicz Park which probably was the difference between winning and losing the game.

I didn't do much practice on my own.

I was training a lot... I used to train with Easkey as well as the county. I'd be doing four or five nights a week between training with the club as well as Sligo. I practiced my frees mostly in club training.

Everything went well for me on the frees in London that day. I remember hitting a long range free towards the end of the game. It was nearly at the halfway line and, at the time, I didn't know how it went over... I didn't think I had the distance.

All the frees were from the ground. I always took them from the ground even when the new rules came in. That day, things just clicked for me and thankfully it helped us get over the line by a couple of points.

We'd a good night after the game in London. We had a drink in the clubhouse and met with the supporters. It was great to chat with them and have the craic.

For me playing football was all about the love for the game.

I enjoyed every time I played and I enjoyed the social interaction after the game. Win or lose, no matter what happened on the pitch we always sat down together and had the craic.

Winning was great but the enjoyment I got from playing football was what I remember most. My county football career ended in 1997 but I played club football up until 2013.

I still love the game!

99

BERNARD MULHERN

SLIGO 0-7 CARLOW 0-7
National Football League Division Four
Markievicz Park
MARCH 1995

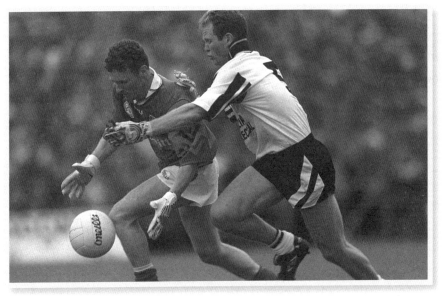

A very late point from Bernard Mulhern earned Sligo a draw with Carlow and promotion to Division Three of the National League in the spring of 1995.

★ **SLIGO:** P Kilcoyne; L Filan, E Sweeney, C White; **B Mulhern (0-1)**, T Breheny, P Durcan; E O'Hara, D Kevany; F Feeney, M Walsh, P Seevers (0-2); P Taylor (0-1), D McGoldrick (0-1), K Killeen (0-1). Sub: M McGrath (0-1) for Walsh.

★ **CARLOW:** P McGrath; J Wynne, D Wynne, J Dooley; B Hayden, S Kavanagh, A Callinan; M Bermingham, D Treacy; K Griffith, J Nevin (0-6), J Murphy; W Quinlan, H Brennan (0-1), N Fallon. Sub: P Meaney for Quinlan.

THE ACTION

IN A LEAGUE campaign that showed so much promise, it was a below-par performance that saw Sligo edge their way over the line and secure promotion from Division Four after over a decade in the bottom tier.

Knowing that they would need a positive result against a Carlow side that failed to sparkle throughout the course of the competition, few expected Sligo to have any difficulty in brushing aside the challenge of the Leinster county at Markievicz Park. But what unfolded was anything but comfortable for home supporters.

Their elevation to Division Three almost slipped from their grasp in a turgid, low-scoring affair, but a late point from Bernard Mulhern spared Sligo what would have been a crushing blow.

A youthful side, with eyes on bigger tests ahead perhaps, found the going difficult against a Johnny Nevin-inspired Carlow, who turned in their best display of the year.

The hosts were met by a stern Carlow defence, and the visitors established a 0-5 to 0-3 half-time lead with Nevin to the fore, kicking a total of 0-6 in all.

With the benefit of the breeze in the second-half, Sligo were expected to move swiftly in front but instead their opponents continued to hold the upper hand and extended their advantage to 0-6 to 0-3 through a Nevin score.

It was 0-7 to 0-4 with 18 minutes to play, and Sligo looked in all sorts of trouble. However, Sligo battled on and the introduction of Martin McGrath helping the cause, as they fought their way back into contention.

The final act fell to Mulhern, who rifled over a long-range point to bring Sligo back on level terms, much to the relief of the home support as the county finally escaped Division Four.

★★★★★

"

IN 1995, I can still remember Mícheál O Muircheartaigh on television when we were going well interviewing PJ Carroll, our manager.

Mícheál said PJ was the patron saint of lost causes!

'No I'm not, this Sligo team has a great spirit,' PJ replied.

And the thing was, there was a good spirit. We had great fitness built up and the big thing was we were winning games.

Promotion from Division Four was key for us – that was the kickstart for some good years for Sligo after that.

We got promoted to Division Three and under PJ in 1995 and '96 we were going well – we let Galway off the hook twice in Markievicz Park. Galway drew with us in two games in the championship, and they came back to beat us in Tuam in the replays.

We lost both… there was no backdoor that time. And I honestly believe if there was, we could have made progress because we'd a great team. We went on then to lose to Mayo in the Connacht final in 1997… another game we could have won. That Mayo team went on to the All-Ireland final again. I've no doubt if we had a backdoor that team of ours would have taken scalps, because we'd a mix of speed, youth, strength, a good playing system… and we were fit.

During my career, we had a few lean years at senior level.

We had some lovely teams, but it was a knockout, and there were some drubbings on the way as well. We got to the All-Ireland B final under Paul Clarke… Leitrim beat us in the Hyde, managed ironically by PJ Carroll. And we got to another All-Ireland B a couple of years later where we played Laois… they beat us as well.

PJ came in then and he had a good record. He had managed Cavan and Leitrim as well.

There's no doubt we had some tough days in the late-80s and the early-90s, but you always kept going because it was an honour to play for your county.

And it was easier then when we started to win games, to go out week-in and week-out, Sunday to Sunday… win in the league, and go for promotion. There was a massive buzz in the county at that time.

Of course, you'd question it at times when things were difficult on the field. But I always kept it going… never drank or smoked, so I was naturally fit.

There were dark days in my earlier years. I made my debut when I was in college in Dublin, and we played Louth. I can still remember going from Dublin to Castlebellingham and playing in the forwards. I scored the first point and the last point of the game… we won by two in the end.

After beating them, you're waiting the next day to get the paper heading into college to see what they thought of it. I'll never forget it; the heading on the paper read… *LOUTH FOOTBALL AT A LOW EBB*.

So that shows you! Sligo weren't rated, and Louth were… and we beat them! That's the kind of stuff that we would hear or see. You have to make your own headlines as a team and when we were going well, suddenly the whole country starts looking on.

PJ Carroll was great. He got us going, motivated us, got us fit, brought positivity… and everyone started from scratch. Everyone was under trial again, even though he knew us as players, as we played against his Leitrim team. He must have seen some potential in us to accept the role.

I remember going up to play Meath in Navan one Saturday. It was a tough game… I marked Graham Geraghty, and it was a great learning curve for us. We came back down after, and the next day we were playing Mayo in Tubbercurry in the Nestor Cup.

We'd two different teams, because he was trying players, but we actually beat Mayo. He brought a few of us on from the team that played Meath in the second-half and, funny enough, I got a goal with my left foot… and I never trained with my left foot! I took a shot because I was under pressure and it flew into the roof of the net.

PJ had us playing Meath on the Saturday and Mayo on the Sunday, and it was a case of everyone having to prove themselves… *who were the dedicated fellas… who were the fit fellas?* The training was tough. Tony Dunne was with him from Ballyhaise, and we'd a great buzz, great camaraderie. We weren't massively into the tactics or anything; it was more about good, hard graft and I have to say, it got the ball rolling in the renaissance in Sligo. I would credit him with the start of it.

We were going well in 1995, especially when we got a win or two under our belt and it really drove on our training.

Training was great, a great buzz and fellas fighting for positions. We were getting a settled team and there was nothing held back in training, it was tough stuff on wintry nights. But you weren't questioning anything because we were on a roll and you were proud of wearing the Sligo jersey.

People were taking note.

When we got that promotion, we took it. But we nearly missed it and if Carlow had beaten us we'd have missed out. It was a massive boost and it was just reward for the work we had put in. Success breeds success.

It's all about the wins; you can have teams there that have near-misses and you lose by two or three points and say you could have won, but when you get across the line it makes all the difference. For example, we went down to Limerick – to play a big, physical Limerick side – and we came out of it just about with a one point victory but that kind of stuff showed there was a winning mentality coming through.

Had we lost that game against Limerick, we probably would have lost to Carlow or some other team.

We went through the league well. The last game was Carlow in Markievicz Park and it was a tricky one. Carlow weren't going great but they had some brilliant players… Johnny Nevin and the likes. A win for us had us in the league quarter-finals in Croke Park.

That time, every winner of every division was going to play in Croke Park, it was a massive thing.

The feeling heading into it was that we probably thought we were going to win the game. It was the last game… we were in Markievicz Park, and I suppose deep down we weren't used to it, but we were probably playing with one eye on Croke Park.

Carlow were mid-table or lower in the table at that time.

Johnny Nevin would have graced any team in the country and he scored a few points that day. We were playing an underdog, when we were well used to being the underdogs ourselves!

Carlow were probably coming in thinking they had a chance to upset the party by knocking Sligo out of getting promotion. It was one of our worst team performances. But going into it there was a lot of excitement… the crowd and the whole lot. The performance didn't match what we were looking for, but we got out of there with a draw.

Definitely, we were getting nervous because we never got into a rhythm, there were mistakes… touching it on the ground, kicking the ball away… missing shots… that kind of a game when you get into a rut and you start thinking… *We could struggle here.* But we just kept going and our fitness and belief probably helped us. We kept plugging away and a sideline kick from my own clubmate Tommy Deignan… he gave it short to me and I went for it from way out.

It went over the bar to equalise the game.

As some of the lads say, 'It's going out 10 or 15 metres every time I tell the story!'

It was probably about 40 metres out. It was out on the left hand side in front of the dug-outs and I just cut inside and went for it. It was against the breeze… it was hanging in the air for a while, but thankfully it went over.

Once we had levelled it, we started to play; another few minutes and I think we'd have taken them. Luckily it went over the bar. It could have easily gone wide, especially on the day we were having and I'd be blamed for missing the shot that could have equalised, so it's a thin line.

We could have won it in the last play of the game.

Seanie Carroll and Dermot Kevany went up for a ball with a Carlow fella. I won the break and was clean through but the ref blew the whistle for a free out; he said they had sandwiched the Carlow man. We could have snatched it from the jaws of defeat completely.

It was a little bit of an anti-climax, but I remember in the dressing-room after; the media and that coming in for the interviews and I remember saying, 'Look, if we were told we were going to get promoted after 17 years we'd have taken the arms off them… so we'll take that!'

It was definitely our goal to get up to Division Three, get up the divisions and start playing better football. That era was the start of it and Mickey Moran came in; he was a brilliant coach and we got to a Connacht final and probably were unlucky in many ways.

We had Mayo on the rack at the end of the final. We were attacking in the last play to equalise and the referee blew the game up. We probably deserved an equaliser but we left it late… we scored 1-2 or that in the last few minutes. Michael Curley from Galway was the referee and he should have at least allowed the final play, considering Maurice Sheridan took about a minute over all the frees.

The team went on after and the backdoor came along and helped Sligo football. But the 1995 run kickstarted all of that and generated an interest in playing for the county. A lot of good players came through in that era and had some great days in the Sligo jersey. It was an honour to line out in the black and white… I used to absolutely love playing. I played in every pitch in Ireland bar Páirc Uí Chaoimh, but my favourite pitch was always Markievicz Park.

I loved going there, the spring in the pitch whatever time of the year it was!

TOMMY BREHENY

SLIGO 0-11 GALWAY 0-11
Connacht SFC Quarter-Final
Markievicz Park
MAY 28 1995

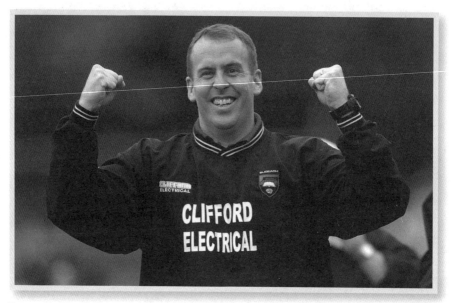

Tommy Breheny believes the summer of 1995 was the decisive turning point in the fortunes of the Sligo team in modern times.

★ **SLIGO:** P Kilcoyne; N Clancy, E Sweeney, C White; D Durkin, **T Breheny**, B Mulhern (0-1); P Durcan, C Shannon; D McGoldrick (0-3), P Taylor (0-1), E O'Hara (0-2); K Killeen (0-1), F Feeney (0-1), P Seevers (0-2). Subs: K Kearins for Killeen, L Filan for Clancy.

★ **GALWAY:** C McGinley; J Kilraine, G Fahy, M Kelly; R Silke, K Fallon, T Mannion; J Fallon (0-2), F Gavin; B Duffy (0-1), K Walsh, T Wilson (0-1); N Finnegan (0-6), V Daly, S De Paor. Subs: A Leonard (0-1) for Gavin; F O'Neill for Duffy, O Hynes for Daly.

THE ACTION

A SLIGO SIDE seeking a first major championship win since 1987 came oh-so-close to both winning and losing this Connacht Championship clash, played in front of a crowd of approximately 4,000 at Markievicz Park.

Buoyed by promotion from Division Four in the league, Sligo showed admirable courage to kick a late, late equalising point through Declan McGoldrick to secure a replay in Tuam.

Indeed, it was fitting that the 29-year-old St Mary's man would slot the difficult levelling free into the breeze, having earlier seen a first-half penalty crack off the post. Had his effort from the spot gone in, Sligo would have been in the driving seat to secure a place in the semi-final.

Starting the game with promise, aided by a fresh breeze, they established a 0-3 to 0-0 lead and the penalty then arrived midway through the opening period, with McGoldrick's well struck effort bouncing back out into play off the post.

Galway rallied from there, and led 0-5 to 0-4 at the break, and with the wind at their backs in the second-half the outcome appeared to be a foregone conclusion.

PJ Carroll's Sligo, though, were made of stern stuff. A young Yeats County 15 – featuring no less than seven under-21s – battled ferociously, with more experienced players such as Fintan Feeney and Bernard Mulhern also showing real leadership.

Sligo held a 0-10 to 0-9 advantage with time almost up, but two Galway scores from Niall Finnegan saw the Tribesmen lead by one into injury-time.

Up stepped the nerveless McGoldrick, however, to send the game to a replay in Tuam Stadium with a delightful curling free into the breeze from a difficult angle.

★ ★ ★ ★ ★

"

HOPES WERE HIGH heading into the spring of 1995. We'd a good league campaign and ended up getting promoted, and we had momentum going into that Galway game. At the time, in the mid-90s, the standard of Connacht football was not at its highest standard, although over half that Galway team went on to win All-Ireland senior medals three years later in 1998.

We had a home game in Markievicz, and if we won, we had Leitrim at home also in the semi-final. Mayo weren't going well at the time, Roscommon weren't either, so really we did feel that there was an opportunity that year to win a Connacht title.

As captain, I certainly had a huge belief in that.

You had several young lads making a name for themselves such as Eamonn O'Hara, Paul Taylor, Ken Killeen, Colin White, Nigel Clancy, David Durkin... all these guys had come on the scene and were good under-21 players, and it really energised the team at the time. There was a good belief there after decent FBD performances and we felt we could compete with all the teams in Connacht.

It was maybe similar in ways to eight years previously, at the time when I made my own debut against Roscommon. At that time, there was a growing level of optimism around Sligo, even though we were rank outsiders in the lead up to that Roscommon game.

We had six under-21s making their debut – there was a nice mix with the likes of Martin McCarrick, Mick Laffey and Robbie Henneberry, so there was a certain amount of optimism, but Roscommon were regarded as firm favourites.

Beating Roscommon that day gave the older players a lift as they hadn't won many championship games in the last number of years and chatting afterwards it was obvious they had fed off the enthusiasm of the younger players, and it drove them on as leaders. I particularly remember the morale in the squad that year with the older members of the team really looking out for the younger players and even though we were young, we had taken a lot of confidence from playing at national level with Summerhill reaching the All-Ireland final in 1985, where you were playing against the best players in the country at our age. We were also competing well against Mayo and Galway in Connacht at underage level; we were very confident about ourselves.

That day, I remember the movement of the McManus's and Paul Earley, how quick and in sync they were with each other. Making my championship debut, I felt it took me some time to adjust to that. We were probably let off the hook on a number of occasions where we had three under-21s in pivotal positions at the back in myself, Martin Keaney and Brendan Kilcoyne playing against a very experienced Roscommon forward line.

The one thing that struck me early on was the atmosphere; there was a big crowd. It was one of the biggest games I had played in. I was very proud to be involved and was really looking forward to the challenge with a belief that we would defy the odds and win. The two Kents were very much mentors of mine – they were a little older and I played with them in the club. I would have fed off them a lot at the time.

John Kent had the sports shop open in Sligo; I used to do a few hours for him now and again. Back then the team was named on a Wednesday or Thursday, and typically it was announced in the national press. So, people would be waiting on the papers to see the team. When it came out and I was selected at centre-back, I was delighted.

That Thursday morning, I was in John's shop. He left me in charge as he had to run across town… and the phone rang. I answered it, and it was a fella by the name of Gerry Emmet. He was a former Roscommon player, who had boarded in Summerhill and was a great friend of John's from Boyle. Anyway, I answered the phone and he asked was John there? I said no… so he says, 'Ah, I was only looking for info on this new fella who is playing centre-back for Sligo… he will get destroyed by Tony McManus!'

I never actually let on that it was me. And he went on to have a full conversation about how Tony McManus would run this centre-back around the place – he was the big name in Roscommon football. And true enough, he was close enough to destroying me because he was very clever, but a couple of things didn't come off for him, and I eventually got to grips and held him scoreless for the afternoon.

I was told before the game if I held him scoreless we had a good chance, so I was glad I played my part.

It was a huge lift to win that game because Sligo had not been winning championship games really, just that previous game against Roscommon in 1981.

That's how much the victory meant at the time, and that's why it has special memories for me. Unfortunately, in the next game we lost the momentum against Mayo.

I broke my hand about six or seven weeks before the game against Galway in 1995. I took off the cast a couple of weeks early just to make sure that I was back and in the frame to be involved, because we had a high level of belief that we were going to win that match.

We really started very well that day – we were all over Galway and were in total control of the game, we were three points up and we got a penalty which would have put us six up. Declan McGoldrick hit the butt of the post and back out... and Galway, in fairness, clawed their way back.

It was a game we could have lost; we ended up drawing it, but we deserved to win it. Nearing the end, we were a point up and the ball came in and bounced on the 14-metre line and over Pat Kilcoyne's head... and over the bar. Pat had made a number of excellent saves before this. Then they got a point in injury time to go a point up, but we went up and got a free to level it. Declan McGoldrick kicked it off the ground.

In the lead up to the game, my memory was of real belief and expectation. There was a lot of excitement about O'Hara, Taylor, Killeen and David Durkin, and genuine confidence we could do it. Leitrim were going well at the time, but we felt that in Markievicz that we had a great chance of beating them in the semi-final if we got over Galway.

There was a bit of excitement too that the winners of Galway and Sligo were going to be live on RTE in the next match against Leitrim – the expectancy was that it was going to be Galway and reigning Connacht winners Leitrim, which was the way it turned out.

There was huge disappointment when we got beaten in Tuam in the replay.

However, suddenly, a sense of belief was emerging that we could compete at a higher level, and while we didn't win the game, it was a good result at the time – there were obvious signs that the fortunes were turning, and I think it really was the start of things improving.

In 1995 we got the draw against Galway and lost the replay. In 1996 we drew with Galway again in Markievicz and lost the replay in Tuam. We got to the

Connacht final in 1997 and then there were the great wins in the 2000s – beating Mayo in Markievicz in 2000, beating Kildare in '01… so 1995 I would have seen as the turning point in the fortunes of Sligo football.

It was obvious there were good guys coming through.

I was 28 or 29, and I was being considered old for a county player whereas now you don't think anything of lads playing at 35 or 36; I see my own brother Mark and the age that he played to at county level and other lads. But back then it was different.

While it was a memorable year, I had started to pick up injuries at the time and I pulled out of the squad the following year, got back for 1997 and played a lot of the league games but broke down again. I probably did not really play much football beyond that. I ended up going into management and coaching at a young age.

But it was noticeable there was excitement with a crop of younger players coming through; that we were on a more upward trajectory and able to compete with the best teams out there, and that was proven over the next 14 or 15 years where we achieved some great results.

Overall, I look back on this game as a turning point in the fortunes of Sligo football and that is why it is a game that stands out for me as captain.

Suddenly, Sligo teams started to believe that they could compete, and there were many memorable wins in both the province – against Mayo, Galway and Roscommon – and big performances in Croke Park in the qualifiers.

And the Connacht Championship win in 2007.

When I went into management in 2006 with Sligo, everything had changed really from when I first started playing 20 years previously.

Back in the 80s, the concept of training was usually centred around running.

That was something that I was probably good at; I prided myself on fitness and stamina, and it would be common enough to go to Markievicz Park training and the first thing you'd do were 10 laps as quickly as you could.

It was always my ambition to lap everyone in the 10 laps! Although it didn't happen. In 1997, Mickey Moran was appointed manager and revolutionised the thinking in Sligo football in so far as training – you could get fit using a football and it was something I very much bought into and advocated. When you become a manager, you probably were a player who had strong thoughts on preparation and I often remember being cranky with managers… running up sand dunes or laps of Markievicz or whatever else.

I really embraced the ball aspect with Mickey Moran and how he designed and planned for training sessions. I always vowed back then if I were to get involved in coaching that there would be no laps.

Things changed dramatically in terms of preparation too. Back in the 80s there would be warm evenings and you wouldn't see a bottle of water; there was little talk of hydration. At the time NCF – when it came to championship time – would come and leave milk at every training session and we thought this was brilliant… professional… *We've made it now because we're getting free milk!*

I recall in 1995, that was the first time we got a Sligo t-shirt to travel to a match, sponsored by Clifford Electrical… we could not believe it.

Diet was another area of revolution. One day before we played Mayo in the championship, we went out to the Ocean Links in Strandhill and had a big steak dinner. This was the way to go; steak was the big thing… it was the chicken and pasta of today.

There was no science behind football then. But you were prepared as best you could be with the tools you had, and everyone had at the time. It is not a criticism of the managers, it was just the way it was at the time. You were nearly discouraged to swallow the water at half-time; you needed to spit it out in case you got a cramp! It's amazing how things moved on so quickly in sport and even the advancements since I was senior manager in 2006/07, where the professionalism and sports science has evolved so much higher to another level again.

I would even have found that when I managed my club St Mary's in 2014/15, seven years on from 2007 – the club scene had nearly gone as professional as the county scene of 2007, things had evolved that quickly again.

PAUL TAYLOR

SLIGO 1-14 ROSCOMMON 1-11
Connacht SFC Semi-Final
Markievicz Park
JUNE 22 1997

Paul Taylor was at his lethal best against Roscommon in the 1997 Connacht Championship (above).

★ **SLIGO:** P Kilcoyne; M Cosgrove, C White, N Carew; B Mulhern, N Clancy, B Kilcoyne; P Durcan, D Kevany; K Killeen, E O'Hara (0-1), P Neary (1-3); D Sloyan (0-2), **P Taylor (0-8)**, G McGowan. Subs: B Walsh for Killeen, P Seevers for Kevany.

★ **ROSCOMMON:** S Curran; S Staunton, M Seely, E Gavin; R O'Callaghan, C McDonald, C Heneghan; T Ryan (1-1), D Duggan (0-1); L Dolan (0-4), A Nolan (0-1), D O'Connor; N Dineen (0-2), D Connellan (0-1), N O'Donoghue (0-1). Subs: D Donlon for O'Connor; T Lennon for Duggan.

THE ACTION

SLIGO BROUGHT THEMSELVES to a first Connacht final in 16 years – and announced their arrival as a coming force – with a fully merited three-point win over Roscommon at Markievicz Park.

Having experienced near misses in recent years, the 1997 success was just reward for a young and energetic Sligo side, expertly managed by Mickey Moran.

Some, however, would be forgiven for thinking that a major championship scalp was beyond the Derryman's charges after the opening 25 minutes, at which point Roscommon had established a 0-9 to 0-3 lead.

Aided by a fresh breeze blowing into the dressing-room end goal, the visitors started slowly with Sligo three in front after the opening exchanges, before Roscommon wrestled control to lead by 0-10 to 0-5 at the break – courtesy of some good scores from Alan Nolan and Nigel Dineen. However, they squandered a number of good opportunities to improve their half-time position.

Roscommon would go some 30 minutes before their next score as Sligo took control. Paul Taylor, stationed at full-forward was having a fine day from placed balls and from play, while his attacking colleague Dessie Sloyan slotted home a 59th minute goal to put the hosts in a strong position, leading 1-11 to 0-10. Youngster Philip Neary also enjoyed a productive afternoon, kicking three points from play.

There was only going to be one winner, it appeared, but Roscommon still had a kick left in them.

Tom Ryan's goal in the final minute of normal time made for a nervous finish, but Taylor remained cool to kick the game's final point – his eighth – and put Sligo through to the provincial decider.

★★★★★

66

I THOUGHT SOMETHING might have been building when we beat Galway in an under-21 championship game in the mid-90s.

We went up to Tuam – Paul Clarke was the manager – and we beat Galway off the field. I thought at that stage there could have been something coming. I think we drew the final with Mayo and were beaten in a replay after that.

Even though we were building, you still had Galway and Mayo – they were always very, very strong. We were certainly waiting on a few players with that bit of extra pace to come along into the team. I think that's where we were found wanting at times in those years, but we did progress fairly quickly.

There were a number of good underage teams that followed each other and that was a big part of it. Club football was very, very competitive in the county as well, and that helped.

PJ Carroll, with Tony Dunne, was a great organiser and a good man to get the best out of you. I think we were lucky from the point of view that we had a lot of good managers, with Mickey Moran coming on board then as well. He came in and he was very different in his approach to everything; he was more of a true coach and I think that's what we needed at the time, and that was the start of the development of that side. Mickey had come from somewhere we all knew, having been in Derry and being successful there as a coach, so he was someone we all looked up to.

We progressed from there as a fairly physical side.

When I look back, there were a lot of lads on that team who were doing physical work as well – and, at the time, that was your strength and conditioning. Peter Ford came in then with TJ Kilgallon and they were extremely organised, coming from a good culture in Mayo.

With the team we had, we always felt we could be successful.

And, as well as that, the camaraderie and fun and craic we had during that time with those panels was unbelievable.

If you went into a dressing-room at that time in bad form, you were done. There was a super bunch of lads there; we all got on well and there was a great bond. That was one thing that really bolstered that team. There was no room for any bit of shyness or that, and we had a good rapport with management.

Our goals were always the same as they are today; we wanted to win that Connacht final. We firmly believed we could do that.

Things just didn't go our way. I think experience had a lot to do with that; most of us were in our early twenties in 1997. That experience didn't really come into the side until 2000 or '02.

Galway were a super team.

We had the measure of Mayo and Roscommon, but Galway won two All-Irelands. They stood between us and our goal to win the Connacht Championship.

I was lucky as a young fella because my father brought me to most games, and I got to see Sligo playing and got to see the Kilcoynes, Fintan Feeney, the Deignans, Paul Seevers and the likes of all those players… I got to see all them.

I played with Sligo from the age of 15. I played under-16 and progressed up through the ranks. When I was 18, I was with Sligo Rovers. I played a lot of soccer with Sligo/Leitrim and myself and Jim Sheridan were actually called in to the Rovers. I was just turned 18 and was out of school.

We were the only two Sligo/Leitrim players brought in. Willie McStay was the manager at the time. I stayed there for two months. It didn't really suit me but I enjoyed the soccer.

I gave it up and Johnny Stenson called me – he was manager of the Sligo team. He told me to forget about that stuff and come in and play for Sligo!

Obviously, I was delighted; it was a big thing then for your club, for your family. You'd have neighbours and club people calling your father and mother congratulating them and I thought that was the great thing about it… it was a big thing for everybody involved and bigger for the family than the players themselves.

I got the call up and went in training.

There were great lads in there at the time – Brendan Kilcoyne, Pat Kilcoyne, the Deignans, Shane Tully, PJ Barrins, Dermot Keaveney… there was a good click of lads there and I suppose myself and Eamonn O'Hara were the new kids on the block. But we weren't that shy either.

We were well able to hold our own when it came to a bit of slagging and a bit of messing, and we probably annoyed them a little more than they annoyed us a lot of the time!

Obviously, training was different, there were a lot of laps.

We couldn't understand as two young fellas – who were fairly fit – how we used to get lapped. We'd be looking at the other lads, thinking they weren't as fit as us, but they obviously had the mileage up from previous years.

The local atmosphere in the build-up to a Roscommon game was always big where we are; there were always a lot of phone calls leading up to the Roscommon games, people wishing you the best of luck and asking you how things were, and making sure everything was alright so that they might have the upper-hand maybe when they'd go to work or the pub that night! They were real derbies at the time.

As players though, we didn't see it like that so much. We'd a job to do on the field, we'd a game plan and that's what we had to concentrate on.

At that time things were a bit simpler; there weren't as many game plans at that time as there are now. I felt at that time football was played with a bit more freedom.

Markievicz Park was full of people.

The roar when the ball was going over the bar… the roar when someone made a good fetch, a good run… the atmosphere was electric. It was electric all the time, no matter what game you had there were always big crowds.

Mickey Moran certainly liked the short game until we worked it up and got to the middle – then you were looking up… looking for the long ball in. That time there weren't sweepers standing in front of you so you had a little bit of freedom. At times, you'd look out and there was too much space in front of you.

Or I'd think there was anyway!

We always thought we could win any game.

We always went into that dressing-room and we had a lot of craic and fun until it was time to stop that – then there was a time to get serious and get ready for what was in front of us.

That group was able to do that.

You had some lads who would rather be quiet, others would still have a bit of craic and then others pulling doors off hinges!

I was full-forward on that team.

I had started playing with Sligo at midfield at underage level. I went from there to No 12 and from 12 to full-forward.

That was the first year I had started to play at full-forward.

I had started playing with the club at No 14 around that time too. Really, a lot of people would have said that I maybe had a little bit of football intelligence in that I'd be fairly versatile in a forward line.

I always liked to think I was a little bit quicker upstairs, because I wasn't as quick in the legs – so my thoughts were moving before my legs were moving.

I was always taught as a young fella to make sure your first touch was good and that you clocked that ball, and that's very important for a player in the full-forward line. If you can play with two feet as well, it makes an awful difference.

I think I got eight points on the day. Philip Neary got 1-2 or 1-3.

From what I remember, we played against the breeze in the first-half but there wasn't a big breeze. We played down into the town goals. It was a real ding-dong battle all the way through.

In the second-half, we relied a little bit on long range free-kicks which I was lucky enough to kick over the bar. Philip Neary had an exceptional game that day; we also won the midfield battle. But the one thing that stuck out was it was our first major step, our first major championship win as a Sligo senior side.

It was a while since we had won one.

There was a lot of emotion from supporters after it – it showed how hungry they were for success, and there was a huge build up to the final. We were very relieved to be in a Connacht final.

I practiced my free-kicks all the time, even from a very young age.

I used to go out into the field beside me after school with two sticks and baling twine and kick the ball over the bar.

When I got to playing at senior level, once that new football came out we used to stay for ages practicing free-kicks. You will always miss some, but if you get away with one or two handy ones to start, your head is in… your eye is in.

There was always pressure on kicks like those too, but thankfully that day they went over the bar and a few more with them.

During that game, there was pressure on and somewhere in the second-half I kicked one wide – and it was an important kick too. The game was level or we were a point down at the time. But Mickey Moran was always one of those managers… I remember looking over at him and he was, 'Keep going… the next one… the next one!' There was always encouragement coming. There was a next one, and thankfully it worked out. In the second-half we did rely a bit on frees, but we got there.

As a player, the result was always the first thing… *Did the team win?*

For me, I was very competitive from a young age. We lived beside a family of nine, the McDonaghs, and we played football all evening and they made me competitive. I was the oldest in my family and they probably helped me to be competitive and get to where I was. They were all good footballers as well.

So, of course, firstly the result mattered more than anything, but I was a forward… I wanted to score. And as a forward, I wanted to come off that field being the top scorer.

It's not that I didn't throw the ball around. I wasn't greedy, and I always felt whoever was in the best position got the ball.

But I was the free-taker, I was a forward and I should have been coming off the field as top scorer every game I played – I was competitive about that.

If I wasn't playing well, if I wasn't clocking that ball, I wouldn't get the chances; if I wasn't preparing properly I wouldn't get the chance to put it over the bar either.

The most important thing was the result, but too many times up to that Roscommon game we might be knocked out of the championship and you'd be out socialising and people might say, meaning well, 'Well it wasn't your fault anyway!'

But it is everyone's fault when you lose!

And it was also everyone's *fault* when we were winning. But that competitive streak was always there in me to be the best I could be.

If I was a forward, I wanted to be kicking scores and until I got the first one I wasn't settled – it was the same up until the very end playing with the club, once I got that first score I was happy and I was away.

I think 1997, '98, '99, 2000… they were all good years for me with Sligo.

We beat the best teams in the country in challenge games, and we beat some of the best teams in the country in the league at the time.

We really were up there with the best of them but probably underachieved.

If I knew then what I know now – and I think everyone would say the same – we might do some things differently. I think it all led to 2002.

I played a lot of football in the full-forward line with Dessie Sloyan and Gerry McGowan. Dessie was the left footer, Gerry was the right footer and I was there in the middle!

We also got on very well, the three of us.

We worked well together and I actually think there was a lot of cuteness between the three of us. If you look at the three of us at club level at the time, we would have been the top scorers for our clubs. We were the three that played for Sligo close to the goal so you were always nearly guaranteed that if one of us had an off day, the other two would do fairly well.

Gerry wasn't too big but he was all there; he had two good feet and once he bagged that ball 30 yards out you knew where it was going.

Dessie then had a super left foot; he had all the power in the world, and he was cute.

And there was the streak in us too – we weren't going to be pushed around. If we got a clip we knew how to give one back!

I was the captain for those years too – and the disappointment then when I was trying to get myself right to play in Croke Park. I took two injections in each hip to play the Mayo game in 2000.

When I look back on the Kildare game in 2001, that was full of great memories. Dessie Sloyan's performance, Eamonn O'Hara's performance… the whole team performance. We were so close. And the enjoyment we got, whether you were playing or not, from that win was brilliant.

It was Croke Park, it was a big qualifier in front of the country. And we progressed well into 2002 as well and that was huge. But I think that Kildare game was one of those games where you could say Sligo had arrived and had achieved something.

PAT KILCOYNE

SLIGO 1-7 MAYO 0-11
Connacht SFC Final
Dr Hyde Park
AUGUST 3 1997

Pat Kilcoyne leads Sligo out at Dr Hyde Park before the 1997 Connacht final.

★ **SLIGO: P Kilcoyne**; M Cosgrove, C White, N Carew; B Mulhern, N Clancy, B Kilcoyne; P Durcan (0-1), D Kevany; K Killeen (0-1), E O'Hara (0-2), B Walsh (1-0); D Sloyan (0-1), P Taylor (0-2), G McGowan. Subs: D Durkin for Mulhern, S Davey for Sloyan, E Cawley for Kevany.

★ **MAYO:** P Burke; K Mortimer, P Holmes, D Flanagan; F Costello, J Nallen, N Connelly; L McHale, P Fallon; D Nestor (0-1), J Horan (0-1), M Sheridan (0-6); C McDonald (0-2), J Casey, R Golding (0-1). Subs: K O'Neill for Golding, D Byrne for Horan.

THE ACTION

A late, late rally from Sligo fell agonisingly short as the county's wait for an elusive provincial title continued after a narrow defeat to the holders Mayo at Dr Hyde Park.

An uninspiring encounter was illuminated in the closing stages by a stirring comeback from Mickey Moran's men – given life by Brian Walsh's goal – though they were left to ponder what might have been had they clicked into top gear earlier.

Mayo, who lost a controversial All-Ireland title to Meath the previous September, failed to match their previous levels of performance but even still held Sligo at arm's length for most of the match.

In front of a crowd of 22,000, Maurice Sheridan was accurate from frees for John Maughan's charges in the first-half, during which they played with the aid of the breeze – 0-7 to 0-3 in front at the break, the eventual winners were still in sight for Sligo, who had points from play in the opening period through Ken Killeen and Paul Taylor.

By the time Sheridan slotted over a 61st minute free, Mayo's lead stood at 0-10 to 0-5 and few, if any, anticipated that Sligo, despite playing reasonably well, would get any closer.

The ground burst into a hive of excitement, however, when Brian Walsh's 69th minute goal, which followed an O'Hara point, brought Sligo to within two, 0-11 to 1-6.

When Paul Durcan fired over a fine score to bring it back to a one-point game 60 seconds later, Sligo's belief levels soared and Mayo looked to be in all sorts of trouble.

However, the Yeats County were left frustrated when referee Michael Curley blew the final whistle just seconds over the allotted 70 minutes, with many believing that a couple of minutes of injury time would have been justified given the stoppages.

★★★★★

"

ALL I WANTED to do was play football as a young fella, whether it was in school or with my club, and every day I togged out I thought it was the Bee's Knees. Sligo was always an ambition too.

My dad had been involved, he played with the county and was a selector in 1975 when they won the Connacht Championship. My grandfather, who unfortunately I never met, played with Sligo for years too, and Connacht in the Railway Cup, so it was in the family and me being stone-mad on football I was delighted to get the opportunity to represent my county.

Sligo were in the doldrums a bit when I came on the scene at senior level.

I made my senior debut in the National League in Tubbercurry against Offaly in 1987, and there were very few at the game.

There were very few at any game that time.

In the early-90s, I was fortunate to play under the management of the late Johnny Stenson and Mick Laffey. They had both won a Connacht title in 1975 – I played with them in my earlier years with the county. When I first started, they were hugely encouraging – they were two great mentors.

In the mid-90s, it built up a little bit more when PJ Carroll came in. He got us fit, and a few more people started going to matches. Mickey Moran came through then and you could nearly count the number of people at a game in Markievicz Park but by the time the following year was over there were 6,000 or 7,000 people following Sligo.

PJ got us fit but Mickey was a man before his time, a great coach; he got us playing a running game and changed things around.

He brought in some young lads that were fast and athletic, and good footballers too; they came through good underage teams. We had some great underage managers in Sligo at that time that got it going again... John McPartland, Leo Boland, Anthony Brennan... good young managers who brought in some great young players.

Mickey took the under-21 team as well, and they won a Hastings Cup, with Noel McGuire and other fellas coming through. O'Hara, Taylor and other lads were classy footballers and they were very athletic, especially O'Hara.

Taylor was a great forward.

Dessie Sloyan, Gerry McGowan… there were some great young players coming through… Mark Cosgrove, Neil Carew, Sean Davey… all good players.

They were a different generation to me.

I played a lot of football with my cousin Brendan for years, a great footballer too, and David Durkin, Bernie Mulhern, Dermot Kevany. The younger guys gave us a lift to keep playing, and it got better and better as the years went on – and then came TJ Kilgallon and Peter Ford and the great days in Croke Park.

I was finished by then, unfortunately.

You thought you'd never see the day we'd get to Croke Park but when the qualifiers came in it gave us a great lift.

We were also getting more games too around that time in the early-90s, because they brought in an All-Ireland B competition and the Connacht League; the more games you're getting the more focused players got on county football because before that it was just the National League and championship – it was a very short season. When it went into a longer season, players got more committed and it became more serious.

We still found it hard to beat Galway and Mayo, but there was the odd great day.

The league structure changed and we went from Division Three into Division One, and we ended up with Kerry and Dublin, Meath and Down as well, and we beat them all… drew with Monaghan and Offaly, who were league champions, so we had some great days.

Beating Kerry in the league down in Tralee, when they were All-Ireland champions, was brilliant. I remember that day, it was the best warm-up we had ever done.

We had nearly the match played before we went out!

Mickey knew we needed a good start so he had us so hyped up and we settled into the game, and we were actually cruising before a fluky goal went in over my head. But I made a great save towards the end – I was never more excited after a league game in all my life!

We beat Dublin in Markievicz Park with a late goal from Eamonn O'Hara. We won by a point, it was so exciting. And great crowds were turning up because we were winning. We were fit, we were playing an exciting type of football, doing things we'd never done before.

In the championship, the draws against Galway in 1995 and '96 gave us belief.

A proud day for me was when PJ Carroll made me captain in 1996 – I remember ringing all the players individually. I rang a few and they were wondering if they were good enough for county or not. But it was about getting the best out of them and we did get the best out of them.

In 1997, the feeling after the Roscommon game was unbelievable. I was never more excited about football.

I had been playing for 10 years – we'd beat London and that would be it. So to beat Roscommon and get to a Connacht final, it was an unbelievable experience. To finally get into a Connacht final and to win.

Taylor was the star that day and Man of the Match.

There was an awful wind but we'd a great start. Mickey used to have us flying at the start of games to get us settled into it. With the wind, Roscommon went 0-9 to 0-3 up and at half-time it was 0-10 to 0-5 but we knew we had the wind in the second-half.

It took us a while but gradually we got there.

They didn't score for half an hour and we went five up, and then they scored a goal. The panic hit then but we got the final point through Taylor.

We'd great belief going into the Connacht final because we had great young forwards and they were unpredictable. Taylor would always get a shot off, whether it was left or right. Philip Neary, a young fella, an off-the-cuff player, got injured before the final unfortunately and that dented us a bit.

The build-up to it was massive.

It was six weeks, which was probably too long in a way, but it kept the young fellas believing that this was our year. We were getting fitter and smarter and had every angle covered. We went up there with great hope.

The hype was just brilliant leading up to it, it gave everyone belief. The flags were out and the papers were full of it.

It was the first time were being talked about on the television.

The bigger the game the better for me... I was even more up for it. It was championship football, and whatever the game, whether it was a final or semi-final with the club or county, the bigger the better and the more hype the better.

It got you more focused. I was probably as fit as I ever was in 1997, probably at my strongest as well.

Mayo were hot favourites and were there in great numbers and we were too, but it wasn't a great game of football.

It was a very dull game but Mayo were a great team – they had been beaten in the All-Ireland final in 1996 against Meath in a replay. They were red hot favourites and I'd say they took us for granted a bit. They were well ahead in the second-half but come the last five minutes we got a goal and two points and brought it back to a point but, unfortunately, time ran out on us. We should have got another few minutes, but the referee blew the whistle spot on the time.

Mayo had great players – two towers in midfield in Liam McHale and Pat Fallon. Paul Durcan and Dermot Kevany did their best. They were probably that bit physically stronger than our younger fellas.

They had Pat Holmes at full-back, who was very experienced, James Nallen at centre-back, Ciaran McDonald at half-forward... a great player. John Casey in full-forward was very fast. We probably defended a bit in numbers that day, frustrated them, hassled and harassed them.

Maurice Sheridan was a great free-taker; he didn't miss any that day... he got six. He kept them that five or six points in front and I was making a save or two as well, so we were hanging in there.

The players kept going and going. Mickey always said if you keep going anything can happen in this game and it did.

Brian Walsh got a goal.

O'Hara and Paul Durcan got points, and we just went for it.

If there was another minute, I think we'd have gotten a draw!

But I probably played the best game of my life.

I made one or two saves that day that you might not make on another day and the young fellas were buzzing, there was no fear in them. We just went out and played and tried to express ourselves.

It was really getting exciting towards the end... the supporters... the black and white everywhere... we couldn't believe it when the final whistle went that the time was up.

When the last point went over, I turned to the umpire and he said we were 15 seconds over normal time! So I thought… *Great, we've another couple of minutes!*

But when the kick-out came it was over.

Everyone knows that Maurice Sheridan used to take time with the frees!

On top of that, John Casey got hurt that day… Dermot Kevany too, and two or three had to go off and subs came on.

If we started like we finished with that running game, who knows? I knew it was my first chance and last chance, whereas some of the younger lads got a good few more chances.

It didn't happen on the day but it very, very nearly did.

After the game I was very disappointed, but proud at the same time that there were so many people there from Sligo that I'd never seen before.

We had that one chance and missed it.

There is that gap there, that you wish you had one Connacht medal, but it is also about the many friends you make.

I still meet them all the time because I'm involved in the GAA all my life. You might only meet a former teammate five times in the year at games or somewhere… but it's like you're meeting him 100 times in the year. You just have that bond!

There's always that bond with guys you played with, no matter who it was; if you meet them at a match you'd always have a chat, there's always that friendship.

And the same goes for players from other counties you'd have played against.

It's the same with your club, though playing for the county for so long it was *like* the club. Just travelling with the different lads to matches and training.

I was travelling in with Paul Severs and Eamonn O'Hara and we'd laugh the whole way to it and the whole way back.

You might be frustrated for a while if you lost – and you'd be giving out about this and that – but then, after that, you'd be laughing soon again!

BRENDAN KILCOYNE

KERRY 1-7 SLIGO 0-11
National Football League Group C
Austin Stack Park, Tralee
NOVEMBER 30 1997

Beating Dublin and Kerry, but especially winning in The Kingdom, in the 1997 National League campaign gave everyone extra self-belief, remembers Brendan Kilcoyne.

★ **SLIGO:** P Kilcoyne; N Maguire, N Clancy, M Cosgrove; R Keane, **B Kilcoyne**, N Carew; E O'Hara, P Durcan; K Killeen, B Walsh (0-2), S Davey (0-2); E Cawley, D Sloyan (0-1), P Taylor (0-6). Sub: K Carty for Killeen.

★ **KERRY:** D O'Keeffe; M O'Shea, B O'Shea, S Stack; K Byrne, S Moynihan, E Breen; D O Se, D Daly; E Fitzmaurice (0-1), L Hassett, J Crowley (1-1); M F Russell (0-2), D O Cinneide (0-3), L Brosnan. Subs: J McGlynn for Fitzmaurice, W Kirby for D Daly, J Brennan for O Cinneide.

THE ACTION

A TRIP TO the Kingdom in the depths of winter gave Sligo reason for jubilant celebrations as they overcame the reigning All-Ireland champions by a point at Austin Stack Park in Tralee.

Sligo's fortunes throughout the early part of the decade saw the county ply their trade in the lower echelons of the National League, but with the arrival of a new cohort of players midway through the 90s, there was a renewed optimism that the county could rise again and contend for silverware.

A change in the league saw an open-format structure adopted for 1997/98, and it breathed further life into a young Sligo team under the management of Derry's Mickey Moran.

A promising Connacht Championship campaign – which ended in a narrow one-point loss to Mayo – was followed by further progress in the early stages of the league that autumn.

Sligo, who finished bottom of the old Division Three earlier in 1997, having failed to win any of their seven matches, produced an outstanding display to secure a historic win against a Kerry side including several marquee names, who only three months earlier emphatically overcame Mayo in the All-Ireland final.

This wasn't a 'smash 'n' grab' win – instead, the visitors should have won by a much more comfortable margin. Eamonn O'Hara and Paul Durcan established midfield dominance early on, and this helped Sligo into a 0-6 to 0-5 half-time lead.

With Sean Davey and Paul Taylor on form up front, contributing eight points between them, the Yeats County pushed 0-11 to 0-6 in front heading into the closing stages.

Kerry threatened to derail Sligo's hopes late on, and a goal from John Crowley via a deflection from defender Ronan Keane made for a nervous finish. Sligo keeper Pat Kilcoyne also produced a smart save to deny Mike Frank Russell.

As the final whistle sounded, there were scenes of great jubilation amongst the 600-strong Sligo crowd as they savoured the county's first ever competitive win over Kerry. It was the second notable win of the campaign, with a late Eamonn O'Hara goal giving Sligo a 2-7 to 0-12 win over Dublin in the opening round. Sligo eventually finished in mid-table, one place above Kerry.

★ ★ ★ ★ ★

66

FOR MOST OF my career, we were in Division Three or Four, hopping around between the two of them, but the GAA changed the league structure then and that gave us the opportunity to pit ourselves against the likes of Dublin, Tyrone, Monaghan, Donegal and Meath. That definitely, in my opinion, gave our fellas great incentive.

People may say you shouldn't need that, but you were playing the Dubs in Markievicz Park and there were train loads of them coming down – it was exciting, compared to going out to play Wicklow with maybe 50 people at it. Suddenly there was excitement and anticipation and it coincided with all these young, better players coming through.

I felt, at the same time, that the bigger counties never gave us the respect we deserved.

I will always remember being brought into Connacht squads for the Railway Cup at the time and myself, Pat and Fintan Feeney maybe would be thrown a No 24 and 25, despite the fact that we made the effort to go for trials and had played well. There was just this thing… you're from Sligo, there's your No 24 and 25.

You have to earn the respect too.

They may have had a point at the time, and it's not easy to say that.

But Sligo weren't at the level Mayo, Roscommon and Galway were at, and we didn't have the tradition or heritage that those counties had – that's just the way the world rolls; when you're on top of the heap you look down.

They were very much like that.

I would've been driven when I was playing with Sligo to always be better, to try and improve and there's no doubt about it, there were difficult years playing with Sligo when we just weren't good enough. We didn't have the players at the time. But don't get me wrong, when I went in at first, there were some fantastic players still around – Martin McCarrick was still there, John Kent, Mick Laffey; they were all coming towards the end of their careers but they were all absolutely quality players.

And then you had a young batch of players that would have played against Roscommon in 1987… Donie McDonagh, David Cummins, Declan

McGoldrick… all these lads that graduated from that Summerhill group in 1985, so there was a team there. But that team broke up very quickly because Martin was at the end of his career, John Kent was the same… Mick Laffey too.

We were left then in a place where we had a very young team and we struggled for a number of years – it was only the Taylors and O'Haras coming through that really propelled it and there's no doubt about it, that rejuvenated me and my desire because we were in a system where we weren't competing at the top level.

We were struggling down in the lower divisions and it was difficult at times.

It was always great fun, don't get me wrong, and I always enjoyed playing for Sligo, but there wasn't much kudos in it at the time.

You knew these lads were coming through.

I don't think anyone stays hanging around a county team on the basis of 17- and 18-year-olds coming through but there was a strong sense there was a more talented bunch of players that we felt were going to rejuvenate things.

There were some great lads involved in those dark years, but we just weren't good enough, it was as simple as that.

In 1997, we got to the Connacht final and that team was so young!

You had O'Hara, Taylor, Brian Walsh, Dessie Sloyan, Colin White, Neil Carew… they were only 19 or 20 at the time, so there was definitely an impetus at that stage but even looking at that team that played against Kerry… Pat was in goals, I was centre-back and Paul Durcan was midfield… and the rest of them were only young lads.

They were just out of '21s' at that stage.

Mickey Moran was in as manager for 1997 and I love Mickey. I still meet him occasionally. You can see what he has done with Slaughtneil and Kilcoo. He just came in and brought organisation, but brought it in a nice way.

There was no bullying.

He coaxed and coached players to get the best out of them.

I know from my own experience that management is a difficult job. We had PJ Carroll before that, and Paul Clarke, Denis Johnson and Tommy Carroll and all these men… they were great men who gave an awful lot up because there was no glamour in it that time for Sligo. But Mickey came in and he was more organised than anyone we had seen before that – the sessions were laid out for us, there was a real sense of professionalism with the set-up at the time and that made players feel better and made them better.

That league game against Kerry came in the autumn time – the leagues were played before and after Christmas at the time – and they were crowned All Ireland champions a couple of months beforehand.

Going down to play them was obviously a big thing.

Kerry, at that time, wouldn't have been known to be taking the National League too seriously but I was looking at their team and they still had Declan O'Keeffe, Seamus Moynihan, Dara O Sé, Eamonn Fitzmaurice, Liam Hassett, John Crowley, Mike Frank Russell, Dara O Cinneide… they all played.

And they were all household names at the time and went on to have great careers in the Kerry jersey.

I just felt, personally, it was one of my better days in a Sligo jersey.

It was one of those days where I was playing centre-back, which is a lovely position to play, and wherever I stood the ball just seemed to drop… it was that sort of day.

That sort of dream day.

My father and mother went down to the match – they were big friends with Johnny Culloty, who won five All-Ireland medals with Kerry. My mother and his wife would be first cousins so they stayed with them and went to the match the next day. I actually came up the road with them after the match, getting back to Letterkenny in time for some socialising, which was a regular match day ritual at the time.

We won by 0-11 to 1-7; it was tight and scary. But just to go down to The Kingdom and beat Kerry, it's just something that gives you a good feeling about yourself, especially when you've come from where we had come from.

The mood was good beforehand.

We had drawn with Monaghan in the previous game and maybe we were lucky to get a draw, we got a score with the last kick of the game. But there was a lot of belief beginning to come into the squad.

We'd a lot of good players. I knew all these lads, like Sean Davey, O'Hara, Taylor, Sloyan and Nigel Clancy… they were all top, top players coming through.

Okay, they were young, but they had absolutely no fear… zero fear.

It was a pleasure to get those few years playing with those lads and it did rejuvenate me because I knew there was something to play for – we're playing the top teams because of the league restructuring and there was definitely a good buzz around the squad. We were in good shape, we were training hard, there was good organisation, the County Board was behind us and everything was going pretty well for Sligo at that stage.

It was a tight game, and while we only won by a point in the end it was one we were always going to win because we controlled it from start to finish.

For a Sligo team to go down to Tralee and do that was phenomenal at the time, and it didn't matter that Kerry had just won the All-Ireland two months beforehand and their heads may not have been in it – they were still *Kerry*... The Kingdom, the aristocrats of Gaelic football.

It created a great buzz around the county.

Success breeds success. If you've a successful county team – take Donegal as an example after winning the All-Ireland in 2012 – young lads look up to that and they want to follow suit and wear a county jersey. Unfortunately, Sligo didn't have enough good times, and that's why we struggle a little bit.

The Kerry people weren't happy.

The legendary Weeshie Fogarty brought me up for an interview after the match, and they weren't happy with Kerry at all.

For the Connacht final the year before, there was a massive Sligo crowd in Roscommon – for a team that had basically 50 at a match three years beforehand. They were now travelling in their droves to matches. There was a great buzz around the senior football team in Sligo during those years. That went on the whole way to 2002 when Sligo had that great run in the qualifiers that took them on to the quarter-finals, and probably should've taken them on further.

For that period between 1997 and 2002, it was a great time for Sligo because people were backing the team, they were liking the way the team played – even though there wasn't much of a system about it at the time; it was basically just go out and play the game.

The game has changed an awful lot since then whereby it's hugely tactically now, but back then it wasn't, it was basically man-for-man, but we played a good style of football because we'd young lads that would run all day.

I was in good enough shape. I'd a bad knee injury in 1995 and I was just probably at that stage getting back to the fitness I should have been at, and I'd a good run with the club – St Eunan's won the championship in 1997 and again in '99 and I was in a good place myself physically, getting myself back.

There was a great feeling of achievement after, I can still see the dressing-room after the match.

Of course, my first championship match, beating Roscommon was a great day; beating them in 1997 as well was another great day, but the Kerry game resonates with me more.

SEAN DAVEY
(& DESSIE SLOYAN)

SLIGO 0-16 KILDARE 0-15
All-Ireland Qualifiers Round Three
Croke Park
JULY 8 2001

Sean Davey in action against Kildare in Sligo's thrilling one-point All-Ireland qualifier win in 2001 in Croke Park.

★ **SLIGO:** J Curran; P Gallagher, M Cosgrove, N Carew; D Durkin, M Langan, P Naughton; P Durcan, K Quinn; **S Davey (0-2)**, E O'Hara (0-1), D McGarty (0-1); **D Sloyan (0-8)**, J McPartland (0-1), G McGowan (0-2). Subs: P Doohan (0-1) for McGarty, N Clancy for Gallagher, D McGarty for Durcan, K O'Neill for McGowan.

★ **KILDARE:** C Byrne; B Lacey, C Davey, K Duane; J Finn (0-1), R Quinn, A Rainbow (0-1); W McCreery, R Sweeney; E McCormack (0-2), J Doyle (0-1), D Earley (0-1); P Brennan (0-7), M Lynch (0-2), T Fennin. Subs: K O'Dwyer for McCreery, G Ware for Sweeney, D Hughes for Finn.

THE ACTION

AGAINST ALL THE odds, Sligo produced one of their best championship performances for a generation to secure a historic win over Kildare in a pulsating Round Three qualifier.

In a first appearance at GAA headquarters since 1975, Peter Ford's side made little of their underdog tag to progress to a fourth round meeting with Dublin at the same venue.

Coming into the game off the back of a comfortable win over Carlow in their first-ever qualifier match, Sligo, in their all-black jerseys, were forced to deal with the early dismissal of corner-back Neil Carew. The Coolera/Strandhill man was shown a red card by referee Brian Crowe inside the opening 10 minutes for an off the ball incident.

However, Sligo showed commendable spirit to battle on with a man less for the majority of the encounter and in a contest that enthralled supporters and neutrals, they clung on for a success that announced the county's arrival on the national stage.

Sligo twice moved four points in front in a good opening 35 minutes, but only led by a point at the break, 0-9 to 0-8.

Kildare erased Sligo's advantage soon after half-time, with Dermot Earley's influence starting to grow for the 1998 All-Ireland finalists. Indeed, the Lilywhites moved 0-13 to 0-10 clear with 20 minutes to go.

Just when it looked like the favourites may kick on for home, Sligo moved up a gear. Powered forward by Eamonn O'Hara, and with Dessie Sloyan in fine scoring form, Sligo upped the ante considerably and scores from Gerry McGowan and Dara McGarty revitalized their effort. By the time Padraig Doohan kicked an outstanding point with seven minutes to go, Sligo were 0-16 to 0-13 clear.

Kildare battled back to within a point amidst a nervous finish, but Sligo clung on for a victory that delighted the thousands of supporters in black and white on Jones Road – and around the world.

★★★★★

66

I CAME THROUGH the Banada set-up and we got to the All-Ireland 'B' final in 1995. Before that, in 1992, they had won the All Ireland with Eamonn O'Hara, David Durkin and Gerry McGowan very influential.

Football in south Sligo was quite strong at that time and we made up the nucleus of the Sligo minor team, along with the likes of John McPartland, Dara McGarty, Phillip Gallagher and Keith Carty. There were a lot of good lads there.

Leo Boland took us at under-16; we won the Manning Cup and went on to minor, and we drew a Connacht final against Mayo in Castlebar.

There was a shocking day for the replay in Markievicz Park. We were winning fairly comfortably throughout the whole game and were two points up towards the end, but a ball came in over the top with a minute to go. It ended up with the full-forward who soccer-passed it by Colin Gordon in goals. That was a heartbreaker.

I was late coming to the game. I was under-12 when I started playing football so I didn't have any real aspirations.

When I came to Banada, I started getting the taste for it – I was at the 1992 All-Ireland, that was actually the first game where I was watching from the stand and thinking... *This is what I'd like to do.* I jumped on the bandwagon and pushed on from there.

I really enjoyed it… the higher level of football, and the physicality. I really enjoyed the physical side of it because I would have been a physical underage player. I was so big for my age, and at county level I enjoyed that, and there were a few good battles in training.

We'd very strong underage teams in Curry. The biggest thing for us was we learned how to win games early – that becomes a habit. If you haven't come from a successful background it's very easy to lose a game, whereas when you're used to winning I find you have a winning mentality; you'll always keep going and you will grind out results.

I would have gone to a couple of Sligo games.

Back then we had a small farm so when I wasn't playing football or training we'd plenty of jobs to do at home. But I went to a few of them. I remember going to a game in the mid-90s when we beat Carlow to win promotion from Division Four. That was a big achievement because we were in Division Four for so many years.

I started training with the team in 1996, but my parents wouldn't let me commit to it until I had done the Leaving Cert. So, I started training with them properly in 1997 – my first game was the Connacht final against Mayo; that was my debut.

The likes of O'Hara, McGowan and Durkin had been brought in, and then they started to look at our minor team. Noel McGuire was brought in too. I was quite young, only turned 18 but it was a big step up.

The game is different now, it is probably harder for a young lad to go in now than it was then because the skill level probably wasn't as high, and the physicality and conditioning levels definitely weren't as high.

A lad coming in from schools' football would nearly be as conditioned as a county player back then, but it's a different ball game nowadays.

The drills we did with Curry or in Banada would have been done to a good level, but I've never seen anything like the complexity and level and variety of drills Mickey Moran had. As a coach, he is probably in the top three coaches I've ever worked under. His drills were second to none.

Every training session you hadn't a clue what you would face; you never did the same drill twice. His training was fun and enjoyable. He was good… a gentleman

The 2000 win against Mayo was my first big win in the Connacht Championship, in front of a full house in Markievicz Park. It was a great win.

We got destroyed by Galway in the next game.

It did and didn't have an effect – we had beaten Mayo and it was a first big win, but maybe we celebrated it a little bit too much as a group and that was a learning curve. Everyone at that time jumped on the bandwagon. The fact that we had beaten Mayo… everyone thought we were going to go on and win everything around us.

But football has a very easy way of kicking you in the backside and we got that the next day against Galway. I don't think we had that mindset ever again – it was a very embarrassing moment as a footballer. I couldn't wait to get off the field that day.

It wasn't pretty.

Peter Ford and TJ Kilgallon came in after the 2000 championship.

They brought a different type of football to it. Peter with his background was a very aggressive player, and he was involved in boxing too so I think he brought us to a different level physically. It was the first time we had an emphasis on gym work, under Peter. It was about lads getting a bit stronger. If you look back on that time, there was a big emphasis on that in Northern football. That was the first time we had proper, serious conditioning training and I think it brought us to a new level from that point of view.

We had some very good days under him, and obviously some disappointing ones too. Our Connacht football was quite poor, but we did really well in the qualifier series.

The Mayo game in 2001 was a poor game, but we actually had quite a good start. We got a fairly fortuitous goal early on through myself, though I tell people of course I was going for the top corner... I didn't miskick it at all!

We'd a decent start and had quite a good hold on the game heading into half-time. But we gave away some silly frees and we let them back into the game handy. That wasn't a particularly good Mayo team, but we let them off the hook. That was definitely one game we let go; we just played poorly on the day to be honest, made a lot of poor mistakes and let them out of it.

But we did learn a lot from that game, and it allowed us to kick on.

We played Carlow in the qualifiers. I hadn't played against them before, but it was nice for me because my mum is from Carlow; she was delighted to be able to go down home and see us play a match.

We won it okay in the end; it was a dogfight for a while but we got through.

When we heard we were playing Kildare in Croke Park, it was brilliant.

None of us had played there before and obviously it's the hallowed ground to go playing on – every kid that plays GAA around the country wants to do that. To be able to run out onto Croke Park was an unbelievable experience.

We weren't expecting it to be in Croke Park. I think Sligo GAA, in fairness to them, might have pushed to get it up there, so we were delighted.

I think it helped raise our performance.

Kildare probably would have played there every year in Leinster. If they were drawn against the Dubs or Meath they'd be playing in Croke Park consistently, so it wasn't a big factor for them. And the fact they had been in an All-Ireland a couple of years previously, they wouldn't have been looking at us as anything serious because we had done nothing to warrant that bar good league performances.

So maybe they took us for granted a little bit.

There were a lot of good characters on that team who had played a lot of underage football at a good standard, where they could hold their own against anybody. If there was a qualifier system in 1995 or '96, I think our minor team could have gone on and won the All Ireland. I really believe that.

Kerry beat Mayo in the All-Ireland final but we would have been there or thereabouts; that's how strong that group was. There was the belief.

We wanted to be on the big stage and probably felt we deserved to be there, but you have to earn it as well. It catapulted a lot of us and we got later success off that because we definitely felt we should be there... we had the work done, we had the ability and it was just about putting it together on the big day.

We stayed in Dublin that night and my car was actually broken into.

Shane Tully took over and he looked after it; he said not to worry about the car, I'd get it back after the match! So that really took the nerves off me... though I'd lost the phone, my contacts... everything!

It was our first away match in the championship where we had stayed overnight. We did it for league football alright with Peter in the year or two previously. So we woke up in Dublin that morning, and we got a Garda escort into Croke Park which was a cool experience. But Peter and TJ knew what to expect; they had us well prepped for the game and obviously we wanted to go win it and be competitive.

We got a good start but then the sending off of Neil Carew was a setback. It was tit-for-tat most of the game, and we got through by the point in the end. They were one of the top teams, but we had no fear of them because we never really played against them.

The sending off didn't really affect us.

We had started fairly well, and you know as a player, sometimes after two or three minutes you might be a point or two up, but you know you're not playing well as a team. This time, however, everything seemed to be going okay, everyone got on the ball early, the touch was good, the pass was good… we had executed a lot of the basics early in the game. It was one of those days.

When Neil got sent off, we continued going well.

We were really holding our own in the middle third of the pitch. Paul Durcan had one of those days. Eamonn was very strong, so we knew if we could hold our own there, we had enough firepower up front to score. It was a day when things went our way.

Just the space of Croke Park stands out for you.

In my natural position of midfield, I felt I had way more space there and you really do, you don't realise how big the pitch is until you're actually on it. It suited my game.

I played a running kind of game and enjoyed that sort of game. I got on the ball early and got my first score off the left foot, and that settled me down.

Back then it was predominantly about winning primary possession. When Kevin Walsh came in we were probably defending a lot more, but back then it was more traditional… 15 on 15! You played your position, and tracking back defending wasn't that big a thing.

Most wing backs didn't want to go up past the halfway line anyway, so it was fine, it made it easier. It's not as easy nowadays!

In the second-half, we got a couple of good scores.

And we were always able to back it up. If they got one, we could get one back and they never got that two or three ahead of us really. It stayed close.

I think we ended up going two points clear with five minutes to go and at that stage you're thinking we might have this. But they were a top team, we wouldn't have been taking the foot off the gas.

The crowd nearly kicked every ball with us in those last 15 minutes.

It was their first time in Croke Park, our first day there – they nearly wanted us to win more than we did ourselves. There was a huge crowd up, it was a massive occasion at the time. All my own family were up… the club! I remember doing the warm-up and seeing a number of the guys from the club senior team; there was a real excitement about the whole thing.

The crowd really got behind us when there was 10 minutes to go. There was a pitch invasion at the end when there shouldn't have been, it was like we had won an All-Ireland but it was an unbelievable experience.

We went on to play in bigger games and went on to win bigger things after that, but that initial game in Croke Park at such a young stage in my career – considering all the other older players who played with Sligo and never got to play in Croke Park – it was a highlight.

As players, you always have to set the bar higher than winning a game, and from there we knew there were bigger games to come. We went there to win the game and move on but unfortunately the result didn't go our way the next day against Dublin.

But it was adding another string to the bow, adding another little bit of belief and sometimes these things take time, and ultimately it did take longer than we thought. But it did pay off, all those experiences and playing in big games.

Ultimately, I think it was a collective experience for later years.

We are probably deemed one of the weaker teams in Ireland – that's a tag that doesn't sit well with me, and as players it didn't sit well with us then and we always felt we were better than we were given credit for.

Any experience like that was money in the bank for us and we knew we were there or thereabouts, if we could get a squad together that was consistent and injury free.

But the experience of big games definitely told in 2007 when the last 10 minutes against Galway was literally backs-to-the-wall stuff, but we managed to eke it out down to all the experience and all the heartache.

It helped us get over the line.

DESSIE SLOYAN

Dessie Sloyan recalls that there was a firm belief in the Sligo dressing-room that they would defeat Kildare in the 2001 All-Ireland qualifier in Croke Park.

"

IT WAS A huge victory not only for us, but a huge victory for the county to beat Kildare and win in Croke Park.

I just remember the occasion, meeting people in the days beforehand. The week leading up to the match, I met a lady who lived down the road from me; she never would have gone to a football match and she said they were all going up to see Sligo play.

I was thinking… *Why are they going to the match?*

But I suppose we didn't get to Croke Park too often, and we didn't realise how much it meant to Sligo people to be there.

We got such support, from everyone… from older people; for them, they were up in Croke Park 1975 and the next time they were back was 2001… 26 years later. Parents were bringing kids up to watch Sligo play, even though a lot of people thought we were probably going to be beaten. Kildare were going well at the time.

We were going in on the bus and it seemed like there were thousands of Sligo people there, which we wouldn't have noticed before. When we got to walk around on the pitch the evening before, it was unbelievable.

Still, people bring it up to us.

If there was a game in my career that I could go back and replay, though, that Mayo game in 2001 is the one. We should have had them beaten out the gate and down the road. That was the year we should have won our Connacht title.

I think Roscommon beat Mayo in the final, but we were flying at the time. I know in Castlebar that day, I missed a goal chance; Eamonn O'Hara missed one, Paul Taylor missed a penalty... and we were still leading at half-time.

Then there was a freak goal for Mayo. Thomas Nallen, their full-back, whom I played football with in St Muredach's, went up the pitch and scored a goal. It was just freaky stuff.

That's a game that always haunts me! Even the Connacht final the year after was there or thereabouts, but I remember thinking we played Mayo off the pitch, absolutely off the pitch... and lost the game.

I don't know how we did it but it was our own doing; we created the chances but didn't take them on the day.

It was strange after that game because we took a break for a week, which was unheard of. We were so disappointed – you're going down the road thinking about going back training after losing this game that we should have won.

It was tough.

We got back together. There was always a great intensity and camaraderie between the lads that were there in those particular years and once we got back together, we got going again. In fairness, the training was never hard at that stage; it was all about football and it was just about getting the minds right and getting fresh for the next game.

We got drawn to play Carlow, which was away, but it wasn't a bad draw.

We would've fancied ourselves as one of the top teams whereas Carlow were a Division Four team, and we were confident going into it and we got over it pretty handy. Once we did that, straight away, we were looking to see who's next, but we never expected to play in Croke Park and I think that was the big turnaround for us.

The big turning point in my career was Mickey Moran.

In 1996 he came in and I played nearly every match under Mickey Moran. He took us at under-21 too.

Paul Clarke was there before him and he was a huge help to me; he brought me in on the under-21 squad. I was a young fella coming in from minor and there weren't too many more young fellas there but he gave me great confidence to come in, and play and keep going that year.

The following year Mickey took over. I was called into the senior squad and I was loving every minute of it, looking forward to going to training… training with the football. Every training session was different, with new drills. He was such a sound guy to talk to and he had an unbelievable knowledge of every position.

He knew what you should be doing and his coaching ability was top class, and he has proven that elsewhere since too. I think he really came to Sligo at the right time to get that group of players and he developed us so much – the combination of him and Peter Ford, they complimented each other so well. Without Mickey Moran, a lot of us would have fallen by the wayside.

There was a good crop of us coming in from underage level.

I played three years at under-21 – the first year we beat Roscommon, got to a Connacht final and drew in the first game and got beaten in the replay in Castlebar. We were very competitive always at that level and probably should have won that final in Markievicz Park. We were a few points up and hit the crossbar. And Mayo came back and got a last gasp free-kick deep in injury time to equalise it. They gave us a bit of a clipping in the replay, winning by six points.

That final was in 1995 and six or seven years later there was a number of those lads on the senior team… David Durkin, Eamonn O'Hara, Nigel Clancy, Padraic Doohan.

Mickey Moran bringing us together and getting a big win over Roscommon in 1997 gave us real confidence, to think… *We've done this at underage now we can go and do it at senior.*

I don't think we ever looked back after that Roscommon win. We went on and didn't play well in the Connacht final and Mayo beat us by a point. But I think that set us up for a lot of years to come, gave us great confidence.

We lost heavily to Galway in 2000, a really shocking disappointment.

We had beaten Mayo before that; we were in great form and played well through the league as well. But that day, against Galway, there was a gale force breeze and we were against it in the first-half. It was also raining heavy and Galway seemed to kick points from everywhere.

We just couldn't get into the game. But I don't think it had any real lasting effect on us, it was just a freak thing. We lost loads of games but that was just a hammering out the gate. A lot of the team changed after that and management changed after that too.

It was Mickey Moran's last game and the following year new management focused everything again.

Peter Ford brought a different dynamic to it; he brought his own style. The first thing he did was work on our fitness – he brought the levels way up.

He absolutely ran us into the ground for a while.

Every night at training, the first thing you had to do was three laps under five minutes and if you didn't manage that you'd have to do it again. Those first few nights, Peter brought us out onto the back pitch in Tubbercurry.

We were doing these laps and I remember a gang of the lads agreed, 'This isn't possible… nobody can do this!'

Peter was after winning an Intermediate Championship with some team in Mayo, so he brought three lads down with him one night for training.

And the three lads did it in the time… under the five minutes! Now, maybe they were international runners, that might have been *the* difference!

But he brought through his own personality as a boxer, as a successful Mayo full-back, as a hard footballer; he definitely brought that to us. A serious professional approach, a lot more physicality to training, one-on-one type of stuff and that stood to us. It might not have worked if we didn't have the football behind us of Mickey Moran.

But Peter coming in changed things around and he built on what Mickey Moran had put in place and pushed us on even more.

The draw was made and we were got Kildare!

Peter Ford rang everybody. He never really spoke to lads individually but that weekend he spoke to everyone and said, 'We're playing Kildare… we've a good chance and we need to get the heads right… there's a chance this could be in Croke Park!'

So then we heard it was there, that it was the real thing.

That's where we wanted to play – the only way for us to get to play there before that was to win a Connacht title. That's how we looked at it for years. It was unbelievable when the news travelled around that we were going to play in Croke Park.

The jersey thing definitely added to it.

We lost the toss but we were delighted with it… we joked about it… the All Blacks.

I still have the picture of the black jerseys hanging up in Croke Park; it was the first time they were there. To me, I would see the Sligo jersey as a black jersey, even though I played in the white one for years and years.

We believed we could beat them. They were a nice team to play, because they played good, open football which suited us. They played open stuff with good footballers, serious players, but we never had any fear of them. I don't remember talking much about them before the game, it was all about ourselves.

Peter would have done a bit of research and told us who you were marking and what style of football they play – but that all kind of went out the window after the first few minutes when Neil Carew got sent off.

You really want to get your hands on the ball as soon as possible, get that first touch and settle into the game. I think we were lucky enough to get the first score. I crossed the ball over to Eamonn O'Hara and he punched the ball over the bar. That was just a relief, to settle into this thing, and enjoy it.

It was a tough day for myself and Gerry inside because after Neil got sent off, they left an extra man back there. In fairness to Peter Ford, straight away he made a switch. Now, it was tough on Dara McGarty but maybe it was the winning of the game in certain ways in that he took off Dara and brought on a defender, Padraig Doohan, to go back for Neil.

John McPartland went to wing forward, where he would have played most of the time anyway, so their full-back just stayed basically as a sweeper.

Gerry and I had a three-on-two all the time and I just remember it being very difficult to get on the ball. We had a game-plan of kicking the ball in early that time.

It was win it, get to halfway… and kick it in.

They always seemed to have an extra man or two and it was tough. But at the same time, the Kildare defence wouldn't be the tightest of defences so once you did get the ball, chances did open up for us. It was a shock to us all, but I don't think it upset us too much when Neil was sent off.

There was no hanging of the heads or anything like that, thinking it was over already. It was a case of… *We have to dig in a bit deeper!*

Taking frees, I would be someone that likes to have something behind the goals to aim at. There was loads behind the goals there, huge stands. I actually found it easier to focus because if there's nothing behind the goals, it's harder to figure out your distance.

But if you have targets… the posts, a net, somebody in the stand you can pick out… and go for as a target… it's better! Paul Taylor had gotten injured the game before, so I knew the free-taking would fall to me a little bit more so there was a bit of added pressure. Paul would usually have taken them on the left, and he would have been seen as the main free-taker and he'd take the ones in the middle too.

I'd always get the odd one or two from the right hand side. That day, I was probably thrown a few extra ones. But I was taking frees for the club all the way up and when you're a free-taker, you want to kick frees.

There was never a feeling that we were home and dry, even when we went ahead in the second-half, especially against those bigger teams. In that game we went a few points up and coming up to half-time they came back into it. And after half-time they went ahead straight away and kicked on.

Peter changed a few things. Dara McGarty came back on and with nearly his first touch he scored a point and I think that gave us a little nudge on again and we came back into it. With that team as well, you had loads of individuals… Eamonn O'Hara, Gerry McGowan, John McPartland, David Durkin, Kieran Quinn, Sean Davey… someone would always do something to change a game for us. I remember Dara taking off, these huge long strides… and he took off and kicked the point. After that, everyone turned around and said, 'Right, let's go… it's now or never!'

We went a couple of points up and they came back at the end.

We took our chances on the day, played well, our work-rate was massive –

everything had built up to that game nicely. We went two or three points up I think with seven or eight minutes to go and I was thinking… *It's too long, we need more!*

It's amazing because, at that time, Peter Ford would have always said to us, we need to score 16 points. Whether it's 2-10, 1-13, or whatever we need, we have to score 16 points to be in with a chance.

We got to 16 points, but I didn't think it was going to be enough.

It was a case of trying to hang on, trying to hold possession. We were trying to do that and we turned it over a few times when there was no need for that. They always had numbers back, which we struggled with all through the game. But in fairness, the subs that came on – Nigel Clancy, Padraig Doohan, Dara McGarty, a few more lads – they brought that extra bit of life to us. Everyone was unreal that day.

It was nearly like winning a Connacht title.

It was strange because we believed in ourselves going up there but at the same time, maybe it was the fact we were down to 14 and the way we won it. I remember supporters running in on the pitch and then they were run off it again.

We went over to parts of the crowd, met our families… people were hugging and kissing. Now, being a lot older and a lot wiser, to see Sligo win in Croke Park, I can understand now why people were so emotional and so overjoyed by it. It's not something you see too often. For ourselves, it was brilliant first of all to go and play in Croke Park, but then to go and win there, and beat a top team in the country as well. We didn't know at that stage whether it'd be as far as we'd go, or where we'd end up. For a lot of us, that was the highlight at county level at that stage.

When you're in Croke Park, you're centre-stage, the whole country sees you. Armagh people and Galway people waited on for our game, they got enthralled in it. John O'Mahony came into our dressing-room before the game too to say a few words; it was all little bits of encouragement.

But definitely that was the day the country said, 'Jesus, these boys are good!'

I'd hold Armagh, Tyrone and Kildare as pretty similar. But looking back, I just enjoyed that Kildare one, the first with the black jerseys. In Croke Park and in front of our own. It was the setting up of that team for the next few years.

99

PAUL DURCAN

SLIGO 1-14 TYRONE 0-12
All-Ireland SFC Round Four Qualifier
Croke Park
JULY 21 2002

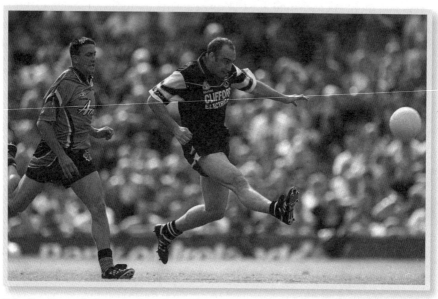

Defeating Tyrone in Croke Park, and reaching the All-Ireland quarter-finals, was Paul Durcan's defining day in the Sligo colours.

★ **SLIGO:** J Curran; P Naughton, B Phillips, M Cosgrove; N McGuire, N Clancy, D Durkin; **P Durcan (0-1)**, E O'Hara (0-3); J McPartland, K Quinn (0-1), D McGarty (0-4); M Breheny (0-1), D Sloyan (1-3), G McGowan (0-1). Subs: N Carew for Cosgrove, P Taylor for Breheny, S Davey for Quinn, J Davey for Taylor.

★ **TYRONE:** P Ward; C Gormley, C Lawn, B Robinson; R McMenamin, C McGinley, P Jordan; C McAnallen (0-1), C Holmes; B Dooher, Paschal Canavan (0-2), D McCrossan; B McGuigan (0-1), S O'Neill (0-2), Peter Canavan (0-6). Subs: C Gourley for Gormley, K Hughes for McGuigan, G Cavlan for Paschal Canavan, O Mulligan for McCrossan.

THE ACTION

SLIGO'S LOVE-AFFAIR WITH the big stage continued in incredible fashion when the Yeats County shocked reigning National League champions Tyrone and dumped them out of the All-Ireland series.

Coming to Croke Park 12 months on from their historic win over Kildare at the same venue, Sligo had a point to prove after a disappointing Connacht final showing against Galway in Castlebar.

Tyrone, with Peter Canavan on song, showed no signs in the early exchanges that they were there for anything other than a routine win, and established a 0-8 to 0-2 lead at one stage in the opening half. Sligo needed a spark from somewhere and got it through Eamonn O'Hara.

The Tourlestrane man, even when Sligo were struggling, stood up to the task and knocked over a point to trim the deficit to 0-9 to 0-4.

Sligo followed on with three points from Mark Breheny, Kieran Quinn and the outstanding Dara McGarty to head into the tunnel just two points in arrears, 0-9 to 0-7. The second-half display from Peter Ford's side was among the best ever produced by the county.

The tide totally went in Sligo's favour – Tyrone only managed three points in 51 minutes after their bright start. Sligo had drawn level at 0-12 apiece heading into the final 10 minutes with McGarty and O'Hara among those to kick points from range.

The knockout blow came eight minutes from time, when Gerry McGowan's left-footed effort at a point from the Cusack Stand side hit the post. Quickest to react was Dessie Sloyan, who rifled a shot to the roof of the net to put Sligo into the driving seat.

Points from Sloyan and Paul Durcan applied the icing to the cake, as Sligo advanced to the All-Ireland quarter-finals.

★★★★★

❝

IT WAS GREAT to get back to Croke Park in 2002. That's where we wanted to be. Even the first year, in 2001, we were hoping we'd get Dublin. Once the draw came out and we got Tyrone, in Croke Park, we were happy… we had gotten a big team in Croke Park. We really didn't fear it. It didn't bother us at the time.

We wouldn't have got to Croke Park had the qualifiers not come in, even though we probably should have won a Connacht title somewhere around that stage as well. But the qualifier system opened it up for us.

We were competing at that top level – we had played Armagh in a National League quarter-final in Longford; we were beaten in a semi-final in 2001 in Galway when Mayo went on to win it.

We should have won that game! A penalty given against Peter Walsh in goals because he used his legs to block a ball! Funny decisions going against you in games like that often affected us.

But the qualifiers gave us a chance to get outside of Connacht and play games outside of the province in championship without the baggage of the Galway and Mayo and the Roscommon teams around our shoulders. And we had a serious team of footballers… like our half-forward line of Dara McGarty, Kieran Quinn and John McPartland. It was a serious line.

At that time, when the so-called experts did the ranking of teams, we'd have always been in and around the Top 12 at the time. That stemmed too from the National League, where a change in structure was a big help to us.

No matter how good you are, when you go to places like Aughrim, or Fraher Field in Waterford, it's only when you play in those grounds that you realise how difficult it can be. Those teams like Wicklow and Waterford weren't a million miles away from us; we weren't far superior to them and our whole preparation had to be right whenever we went there.

Everything had to be spot on.

When you go up against Dublin or Kerry, you have nothing to lose; you try things and they might just happen for you and, all of a sudden, that brings its own confidence. That happened in the late-90s. But even since, loads of people have said it to me, there was a serious panel of players there.

I wouldn't say as a young fella growing up that I was dead set on playing for Sligo.

I was like anyone, if the rugby was on television we'd go out and play that... if the tennis was on we'd do the same. Minor was the first time I played for Sligo, at corner-back.

I was at trials for the under-16s; there were four or five of us there from the club and I was the only one who didn't make it. Even when I'm coaching the young lads here in Curry now, I tell them that if it doesn't work out first time, it doesn't mean that it won't work out at all.

I was lucky enough that I was born on a farm and you'd be out farming, lifting things and working on your strength; the same things fellas are doing in the gym now. I was into running at the time too. It kept me fit but it wasn't until I was 18, in 1988, that I made the minor team for Sligo.

My early football was all in the backs.

With the club, I started off in goals as a 10-year-old and then progressed out to full-back. I played centre-back, corner-back, wing back, wing forward... in all of those positions for the county. My level of fitness was very good at the time; technically I wasn't as gifted but I had the staying power for the middle third, so that's probably why I ended up out there.

The thing about midfield is, it's a hugely physical part of the field.

It's only when you come into your late-twenties that you fully develop the stature necessary for that area. You're up against big, big men all the time; every time we played teams there was always someone at six foot five or six, no matter who you played.

I remember playing Wicklow... they'd two big huge men, Cavan the same. Mayo had big midfielders, most counties had big fellas.

The likes of Taylor and those lads were coming through a couple of years after I started at county level.

Johnny Kenny was playing with us that year as well, and we pushed Mayo to four points – and they were always being touted to win Connacht. So, there were little glimmers like that, but then you'd go out the following day and get annihilated and it'd knock you back.

We might go down and play the likes of Waterford in the league and we'd get beaten. That was where we lacked the bit of consistency in backing up a good performance with another one.

During the 90s, I actually came very close to pulling away from the county scene. Even at the start, in 1990, I was in America for the summer and I came home for the club semi-final and final. When I was over there, I had applied for the visa, and at that time when you got the forms back for the visa there was a fair chance you'd get it. I was very close to going back again but then I got in on the county panel… and next thing I got working in a meat factory… then I got the job coaching for a while. That kept me here.

In 1994/95 I wasn't getting much game time, and I came very, very close to packing it in.

I was talking to the lads in the club at the time and they told me to stay in there, to stick at it. I did, but there was a row one night; I didn't go to training and there was a row between two men and they fell out. I played against one of the men then at the weekend for the club and we ended up boxing each other – and I got on very well with the same man – but when the game was over we went over to Howley's and when I opened the door there was the pint for me!

But PJ Carroll got a hold of this row that took place and, next thing, I was back into midfield. It was funny, but that's how it happened.

PJ came in having been with Leitrim. He had a reputation of getting things going and we also had the younger talent coming through too, off the back of Banada winning the All-Ireland. I was involved in coaching at the time too – we were in all the national schools and all the secondary schools. The coaching was well organised throughout the county.

Like Banada and Summerhill competing for Connacht titles and All-Irelands, the Vocational Schools were competing at national level for titles too. So, it was beginning to turn a small bit. The under-21s made a Connacht final, and then we had the minors in 1996 and '98.

We could see there was something happening. Being involved in the coaching, I could see it out there on the field as well.

Roscommon in 1997 in Markievicz… we were never expected to win that.

Galway, Mayo and Roscommon were always expected to beat us and Leitrim at the time were going well too – in 1991 I actually made my championship debut against Leitrim when we had a 16-point hockeying up in Carrick-on-Shannon.

We'd a nice team in 1997.

Philip Neary kicked 1-2 that day so there were some good young lads. Sean Davey had come into that team as well, all the lads were coming in off the minor team in 1996. That was the first real breakthrough, and we were hoping then to go and build on it.

Even then in the Connacht final, we left it very late to come back and there was only one in it in the finish. The thing then was to come back and build on it the year after – that was always our biggest issue.

Mickey Moran brought in a whole different type of training.

He was big into drills, all different ones. We did a lot of running with PJ but Mickey was *everything* with the ball. Maybe we needed a bit more physicality, more running but his coaching was totally different to what we were used to in Sligo.

A lot of clubs actually came in to watch him doing the training and brought that away with them.

The Connacht title wasn't put up there as the be-all and end-all, but it would have been nice personally to get a medal.

They're hard got, no matter what county you're from. But, I suppose, we still knew that we were plying our trade fairly well in the league and that we were capable of beating anyone. The bigger team we got in the draw, the better for us.

The 2002 Connacht final is a big regret. It's amazing, I'd remember more about those days than the days against Kildare or Tyrone. Just little things that I did wrong myself, they still come back and haunt me.

The goal that day… I can remember it as if it's happening in front of me now because I missed a tackle and one second later it was gone… back of the net! They're the games I'd remember more than the games we won.

Watching the 2002 game against Tyrone back during lockdown last year, there's one image that floods back.

I was sitting in the dressing-room at half-time saying that we have this game turned. We were still losing, but I remember saying that to the lads. They had thrown everything at us and we had soaked it all up and going in through the tunnel, I had this in my head… *We have this game turned.*

Just that air of confidence.

Myself and O'Hara were always midfield, even though himself and Kieran

Quinn used to swap in and out a little bit.

For me, if I got up the field to have a shot at goal I was happy enough. My whole game was fixed on blocking spaces and covering back, being a link and a cover, that's where I spent most of my time through the years. Technically I probably wasn't as good as the rest of the lads.

Later on, I would have spent, even through my coaching, more time doing ball work. I was 33 or 34 before I scored with my left foot!

When I started off there was no practice – the coaching has brought things on a lot. But most of my career would have been spent being a bit more defensive, organising, that sort of stuff, shouting at fellas to come back... 'GO LEFT... GO RIGHT'... all that.

At that time, the kick-outs were just hammered out there and it was just do what you can.

When Dessie got the goal that day we went ahead, but when you're in the moment you never think you have the game to lose. I never thought like that, and until I heard that whistle I knew it was never in the bag. I'd be still full-on into everything.

The Kildare win was probably more of a ground-breaking win, and the Tyrone one was more about that consistency that I talk about. It's hard to say it's a back-to-back performance. It was our third game in Croke Park, and it really was a case of... *Yeah, we can do this!*

It doesn't matter who we play... *We are good enough!*

And we were – we had a serious, *serious* team.

We came up against Ulster opposition in Armagh, who were probably further up the road in terms of preparation; they were getting stuff from Rugby League and stuff like that, and they were a more professional outfit at that time than any other team.

Could we have won the All Ireland? When I ask myself that question, I always think of the day we went out and beat Kildare, and then went out against Dublin and got beaten by 16 points. You cannot say we would have gone on to win the All-Ireland. We had the capabilities, but to go out and do it consistently, we hadn't done that.

We wanted to win Connacht Championships, so we were trying to put two or three games back-to-back. To win an All-Ireland you have to be consistent because there is a day you'll go out and things won't happen; so you've got to just get through, manoeuvre your way through the game and get a result.

If you look at the good teams, even back then, Armagh weren't beating teams by a lot but they were getting over the line. Even the day against us, they were just able to do enough to see themselves out. That comes with a lot of time and effort, and good organisation.

We had a panel good enough to get there, but when you look back we were missing Paul Taylor for a lot of those games as well. Paul was a huge loss for us, even though he did come on against Tyrone.

I'd an aunt who died of cancer.

When she was on her deathbed, she called us all in. She said to me, 'My wish for you is that you'll play in Croke Park'.

That was in September of 1996. And then, I'll never forget it, we were making silage the day it was announced we were playing Kildare in Croke Park.

It was like a dream, a wish... a prayer come true.

So, to beat Kildare in 2001, and then Tyrone in '02, in the biggest ground of them all was a great honour for a footballer from Sligo.

JOHN McPARTLAND

SLIGO 0-17 ARMAGH 1-16
All-Ireland Quarter-Final Replay
Páirc Tailteann, Navan
AUGUST 18 2002

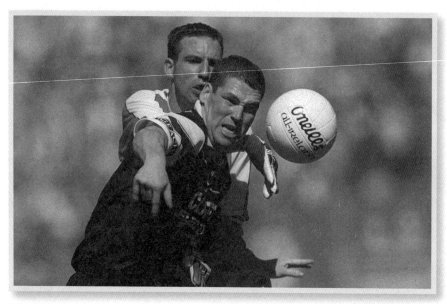

John McPartland wins the ball against Armagh's Enda McNulty in the 2002 All-Ireland quarter-final replay.

★ **SLIGO:** J Curran; N Carew, N Clancy, B Phillips; N McGuire, P Naughton, P Doohan; P Durcan, E O'Hara (0-2); K Quinn, **J McPartland (0-3)**, D McGarty; D Sloyan (0-9) S Davey (0-1), G McGowan (0-3). Subs: M Langan for Carew, M McNamara for Durcan, K O'Neill for Clancy.

★ **ARMAGH:** B Tierney; E McNulty, J McNulty, F Bellew; A O'Rourke, K McGeeney, A McCann; J Toal, P McGrane (0-1); R Clarke (1-2), J McEntee, O McConville (0-7); B O'Hagan (0-2), D Marsden, S McDonnell (0-5). Subs: J Donaldson for McCann, T McEntee for Toal.

THE ACTION

A GLORIOUS SUMMER came to an emotional end as Sligo came up agonisingly short in a pulsating All-Ireland quarter-final replay against Joe Kernan's Armagh.

Having salvaged a draw from the jaws of defeat in Croke Park a fortnight earlier – when they came from six points down – Sligo very nearly repeated the feat in Navan, having fallen seven behind in the early stages of the second half.

Trailing by two at the break, 0-10 to 0-8, Sligo found themselves in all sorts of trouble after Ronan Clarke netted an all-important goal for Armagh soon after half-time.

Indeed, the best goal chance of the game up to that point had fallen the way of Sligo, but Gerry McGowan's effort was blocked by Kieran McGeeney in the 13th minute of the opening half.

This was a Sligo team full of gusto, and backed by their vocal support they surged back into contention.

With Eamonn O'Hara driving the team on and John McPartland growing in influence around the middle third, Sligo continued to make a dent in the arrears as the game entered the closing stages with Dessie Sloyan as scorer-in-chief, kicking 0-8 – all from frees.

Wastefulness, however, marred a power-packed Sligo performance. Six second-half wides hindered their cause, but there was still time for one final twist.

Trailing by two, Sean Davey appeared to be fouled in the Armagh penalty area in the closing stages when he was surrounded by three defenders – but referee Seamus McCormack waved play on. And so ended Sligo's odyssey.

★★★★★

66

FROM 1999 TO 2003 or so, there was a serious team there and it's only when you look back now that you realise that.

Although we trained as hard when there was no backdoor, I think the backdoor created a bit of a buzz for Sligo. In 2001 we played Mayo in Connacht and we should have won that game, but we then went on to play Carlow in a qualifier and we got to Croke Park to meet Kildare and Dublin.

There was a real togetherness too with the supporters, and that was because of the backdoor. It was also different – we were playing different teams and that gave it a bit of a buzz.

We got to a National League semi-final in 2001, when we were beaten by Galway in Hyde Park. We were playing in some big games and that brings everything on too.

Peter Ford came in after Mickey Moran and he was top class.

We had massive respect for him; he was a player's man but he was the boss too. We were very fit – he came in with Jarlath Cunningham and TJ Kilgallon. But there was enjoyment too and, of course, a serious core of players.

All that said, in the lead up to 2002 we had some difficult days as well.

I can still remember a good bit of the Galway hammering in 2000. Actually, I'll never forget that day – I got the first ball that came up and I thought… *This is going to be a good day.* But sure, it was the only ball that came up after that.

Everything they had, they kicked. But I also think we thought we were better than we were. I was working in Dublin at the time and I got the train back up on the Monday morning. There were two older ladies giving out about Sligo football and I just kept my head down!

In 2001 we had more chances to beat Mayo in Connacht.

We missed a penalty too, but the only good thing about losing was that we had a game to look forward to two weeks later in the qualifiers, as opposed to waiting around for the following year.

We went down and beat Carlow and then we were waiting to see who we were going to get in the draw. It came out that we were to play Kildare, and the rumour started that we were going to be in Croke Park.

It was unreal when we were going there… and then to win there!

The biggest thing about 2001 and '02 – although we won nothing with that good team – was beating Kildare. It took us another step to the following year where we beat Tyrone, and nearly got the better of Armagh.

When we got to 2002, there wasn't much talk of aiming to win Connacht.

After losing to Dublin the previous summer, we ended up meeting up during the winter every week or so, and we'd have programmes to do. We were then tested on a Saturday.

Everyone was training on their own. I was in Celbridge doing it – we had gym programmes back then too. After beating Kildare, losing to Dublin and getting a taste of Croke Park, there was definitely an added motivation to get back there and see what we could do.

Our first game in the championship was against New York.

It was one we were worried about because we were the first team to go out there and play. A few weeks before, Peter Ford and Padraig McKeon went out there to look at the pitch, look at the hotel and training facilities… nothing was left to chance.

As I said, we didn't really focus on winning a Connacht title. There was a good panel back then but at the same time, we never thought we were world beaters or that we were the best, we just aimed to work hard each game.

In the Connacht final, when we went at it, we performed in the last 20 minutes. I suppose after that disappointment we needed a good draw – we got Tyrone. After the Galway game, we had played Tyrone and Armagh in two friendlies before the draw was made. Playing good teams all the time brought us on.

Of course, it was brilliant to beat Tyrone, but we didn't realise at that time what sort of team they were. We were delighted to win, but it's only looking back now that you appreciate it that bit more; when you see what they went on to achieve.

The day before the Tyrone game, we were in Croke Park for a look around, laughing and joking… and they came in at the same time but were completely different, very business-like. But we managed to get the win.

Then it was on to Armagh.

For me, there's more regret about the replay against Armagh than the drawn game.

The second day, we conceded a goal after half-time and went six or seven down. We had three or four chances for points we didn't take, we gave away ball… could have scored a goal in the first-half. The drawn game we had chances to win but losing the replay always wrecks my head, even now.

Nowadays it's different – when an underdog draws a game, usually they are disappointed. But in 2002, there was no disappointment in our dressing-room. The whole team stayed up in Dublin after the game and the atmosphere was good.

We went to Navan the week before the replay to do a bit of training on the pitch. I think Armagh got us out of Croke Park, they didn't want to go back there.

We went up the night before.

The game was at six o'clock but there was a lot of stuff organised for us, team bonding and that to pass the time. However, when we were going to the ground, we had to change route because Sligo supporters had taken over the town.

We were confident in our abilities going into the replay.

It was a team with no real standout player, but there was a work ethic, and we had seriously big men, strong fellas. In training there were a lot of physical battles.

It was a seriously hardworking team and that is what Peter put into us. In the half-forward line where I was, we were told to work, work… work. And if you can't keep going put your hand up and come off. There was serious craic too, even before the Tyrone or Armagh games there'd be a bit of craic but when it was time to be serious, it was serious.

There was no fear that day… no fear.

We went three points up early on, but then they came back and scored four or five. It was fairly high paced stuff.

There was a lot of space, a lot of space to be got at in that game. We were two points down at half-time but at the start of the second-half we gave away 1-1 or something like that and there was a lot of ground to make up after that.

We got it back to two points by the time Sean Davey had the shout for the penalty. I don't think about that so much – I think more about the ball we gave away and the chances we missed more so. If we got the goal in the first-half, maybe… but that's football.

I watched the game back during lockdown last year and to tell the truth, it still hurts, even 19 years later. They were very physical, especially in the drawn game;

they got away with a lot. But we matched that, we had no fear, as I say.

They were a big and direct team, and it shows how good a side they were to go on and beat Dublin and Kerry.

The support was unreal, and I always go back to that – there was a connection between the team and the supporters. It's one of the big things I take away from 2002.

I don't know if it was the qualifiers or not, but the crowds, the Croke Park days... there was a massive buzz. Drawing with Armagh, the noise of the Sligo supporters after was unreal. Even in Navan, the crowd chanting, 'SLIGO... SLIGO' when we were coming off the field, it was unbelievable.

But unfortunately, nothing came off it.

The dressing-room after was a disaster. We had stayed out on the pitch for a while but there were a lot of tears from supporters and players. It was a lonely journey home.

We'd a good chance of going further.

I would have liked to have gone one step further and see what would have happened. But you can't really say what we would have done, whether we'd have beaten Dublin in Croke Park and reached a final.

It was one of the best teams I played with that won nothing.

I was lucky that I played and got a medal in 2007 but there were a lot of lads that played that time that have no medals to show.

We certainly could have won something with that team.

EAMONN O'HARA

ROSCOMMON 2-5 SLIGO 0-13
Connacht SFC Semi-Final
Dr Hyde Park
JUNE 17 2007

Eamonn O'Hara celebrates with the Nestor Cup in the Sligo dressing-room in 2007, but the semi-final win over Roscommon was the game that truly defined the midfielder's' summer.

★ **SLIGO:** P Greene; C Harrison, N McGuire, R Donovan; P McGovern, M McNamara, J Davey (0-1); **E O'Hara**, K Quinn (0-1); B Curran (0-3), M Breheny (0-4), S Davey (0-2); D Kelly, P Gallagher, A Marren. Subs: J McPartland (0-1) for Marren, K Sweeney (0-1) for Gallagher, G McGowan for Kelly.

★ **ROSCOMMON:** G Claffey; S McDermott, A McDermott, P O'Connor; S Daly, D Casey, R Dooner; S O'Neill, M Finneran; J Tiernan, G Cox (0-1), C Cregg (1-0); D Connellan, K Mannion (1-1), G Heneghan (0-3). Subs: A Murtagh for Daly, E Kenny for Tiernan, D O'Gara for Cregg, D Keenan for Doonan.

THE ACTION

AFTER A COMFORTABLE opening round win over New York, Sligo passed the first real test of their championship credentials with a deserved two-point win over Roscommon at Dr Hyde Park.

In what was the county's first win over the hosts at the Roscommon town venue since 1971, Sligo produced an outstanding second-half display to edge their way into the provincial decider.

An encouraging start gave Sligo an early advantage, with Kieran Quinn's point from play a highlight of the opening stages.

In what was a first-half low on quality, Roscommon hit the front when Karol Mannion netted – having kicked a good point from play to get the home side motoring – and they went in at the break 1-3 to 0-4 ahead, with Sean Davey's fine effort before half-time helping Sligo's cause.

A purposeful start from Roscommon in the second-half, however, suggested Sligo's title ambitions would perish at the semi-final stage. Cathal Cregg blasted home a goal a mere 90 seconds after the resumption, and Roscommon were suddenly firmly in the driving seat.

However, Tommy Breheny's men had other ideas.

Gaining a greater foothold at midfield through Eamonn O'Hara and Kieran Quinn, Sligo began to dominate the remainder of the game. John McPartland and Kenneth Sweeney both pointed after their introduction, while Brian Curran's direct running caused the home side all sorts of trouble.

Roscommon simply had no answers, and Sligo hit the front 10 minutes from time when Mark Breheny floated a point over from 45 metres out – 0-12 to 2-5 in front, Sligo lived dangerously and Roscommon had a good chance in added time, but Michael Finneran's attempted shot went right of Philip Greene's left-hand upright.

Sligo got their insurance score – fittingly from the industrious Brian Curran – to seal victory and set up a tilt at Connacht glory.

★ ★ ★ ★ ★

66

THE 2007 GAME against Roscommon, the Connacht semi-final, is one that sticks out for me.

Even though we were dominated in the general game, I felt I was in a position where I was doing well – my reading was good, my timing was right, I was playing midfield and things were good. In the second-half, my contribution to the general game was so much better... we dominated the second-half.

Mark Breheny and Brian Curran were brilliant. Brian kicked scores that he'll probably never kick in his life again.

When Peter Ford came in, we really started to think about Connacht titles.

Peter was a lovely guy, but his self-confidence... people might describe it as arrogance but it's not. It's a self-belief moulded by confidence. He couldn't believe why we would not be thinking like Mayo; he just could not understand it.

When he started out, he was asking, 'Why do you not think like a Mayo person? Why do you undervalue yourself?'

We'd often have those conversations with him when we'd have a night out and he'd open up a bit. He just couldn't understand it and then that sort of streak came within us, where we said... *We're here to stay!*

When we started out we played Kildare in Croke Park and you had the whole thing with changing the jersey from white to black – they were saying, 'Right, this is only for a once off!' but Fordie said under no circumstances were we changing back.

We were all in agreement with him and you could see his way of doing it was the way we needed to go about our business.

We're not taking any nonsense here!

Maybe we were getting a little bit arrogant ourselves. We weren't winning anything, but it was... *We're here... we're not going to be dictated to by anybody.*

I think that's when the real self-belief came in.

We were in an era in 2000, '01, '02, '03, when we played against all the All-Ireland champions of that time.

We beat Tyrone... they went on the following year to win it.

We could've beaten Armagh in 2002.

We played Galway, the 2001 champions, in the 2002 Connacht final in a game we didn't play in at all and we only lost by a goal.

We were very, *very close*… we had that bunch of fellas from the 1994 era who had come through and we were all coming into our peak years. We were ready to win something.

Tommy Breheny took over in 2006.

I obviously knew Tommy well. He was captain and I was vice-captain in 1994, so we worked well together. He gave me great advice at the time, not to play the occasion and all that, but unfortunately, he retired young. But he was still very ambitious. He managed St Mary's; he knew the club scene inside out.

He went in there with John Kent, the two of them were brilliant. Every message was about how we were going to win a Connacht title, and funny enough when you keep saying something like that you start to believe it.

If you keep saying you're no good, you will be no good.

But if you keep saying you're going to be successful, you might start believing it. Myself and Gerry brought that in with our philosophy in Tourlestrane, that we're doing this to win, we're doing this to be successful and to be winners. And that shows how far Tommy and John were ahead in their thinking at the time.

We needed the players too, of course. We had a few lads who were in and out and at different things, but we got the full commitment from everybody and they put a team together… and it just clicked and happened.

We went over and played New York and a trip to New York is always brilliant, but we had never stayed on. We usually would end up coming home on the Monday evening, but this time we ended up staying until the Wednesday or Thursday. My God, it was the best four days of everyone's life, it was great craic.

We did have fun, but the training we did over there was hard.

I think I got a goal early in that game, and it gave us a bit of a base and we ended up winning well so it wasn't one of those games where you'd be absolutely buckled sore or anything else… and we had all the gear!

Teams that went to New York before us and afterwards had suits and shoes… we ended up getting Dunnes Stores and white Penneys shirts and someone else got a raft of ties and we threw them on anyway! But that's what we had over there!

We trained as a group, not that we did anything too hard but it was intense, it was focused; we went into the gym a few times and we just had great craic. It was a great bonding session with each other.

The first-half against Roscommon was poor.

We went in full of conviction that we were going to win, simple as that.

It was the first time going up there thinking... *We're going to beat Roscommon here.* That was never there in teams before; we'd almost be apologizing for saying we've a chance to win it, but we were thinking we were going to win... we were going to do what we needed to do. We had our homework done on individuals, had done everything we needed to do, but we just didn't perform to the level that we should have.

Second-half we just clicked; we kicked on and were exceptional.

We always felt we could beat Roscommon and even down through the years we always had good games with them. We never got hammered by Roscommon... we got hammered by Mayo and Galway many times but never Roscommon. We just believed we could compete with them and we did. There were some classic games between us; the players knew each other inside out.

We were never deemed as being up there, whereas Roscommon had history against Mayo and Galway and had won Connacht titles, but we never had any history because we were never in the mix.

But we tried to get ourselves in there even though a lot of the top teams would look at us as a 'nuisance team' more than anything else, thinking... *They'll stick with us for 40 or 50 minutes and we'll beat them in the last 10 minutes.* That was the way we were viewed and that was the way a lot of the time it panned out.

We just didn't have the depth of quality, but this time around we had it in 2007 when Tommy was able to make a few changes.

A lot of lads stepped up and played exceptionally well. Patrick Naughton was outstanding in New York, and Brian Curran and Mark Breheny were outstanding in Roscommon, so it just shows you at key moments, we weren't looking to one or two guys to be the leaders, somebody else popped up that you may not have been expecting. That was the character of the group.

We weren't favourites. It was Tommy's first year in and we had an indifferent enough league – we had to beat Wicklow in the last league game not to get relegated so it's not that we had a smooth sailing through the league, but the training we were doing in the collective group was good and we had some really, really good challenge games. It just set us up so that we were in the right form.

I think there was more balance in that team.

Physically we had stronger players... we had Paul McGovern, Michael McNamara, Brendan Egan; and Kenneth Sweeney was coming to the party and even though he wasn't starting he was coming on and able to kick two or three points.

Mark Breheny was in a rich vein of form. Johnny Davey was there .. Noel McGuire was outstanding at full-back. John McPartland was very physically strong, Kieran Quinn was another option from kick-outs. We had that blend of players that you could say, 'Yeah, we're able to compete with the very best and physically we're able to compete with anyone'. Football wise we'd equally skilful players... and that's what it was.

Now, I wasn't foolish enough not to know that Connacht football at that time was probably on the way down a little bit. Even though Galway had won the All-Ireland in 2001 they never kicked on from that, and Mayo were in a bit of a transition period. So we had a chance.

Truth be told, we probably should have dominated that era in terms of getting Connacht titles, which is a bold statement, but the opposition just wasn't there.

I think we just hyped ourselves up a bit.

We went out in the second-half and it was a case of now is the time to put the shoulder to the wheel, and really we put in a performance and it sort of clicked for me in terms of being involved in the game and being physically strong.

I was marking Seamie O'Neill, and I was able to bully him in a way... being competitive, breaking up the play. I was reading it right and the pace was right, that type of thing. Then Mark and Brian really stepped up and kicked the lights out.

I suppose you get to a stage in your career where you realise you can lead by example, or you can talk a big game and then not deliver.

There were so many leaders in the group who could have been captain – Michael McNamara, Paul McGovern, Charlie Harrison, Ross Donovan, Kieran Quinn, John McPartland... we had enough lads who were leaders in their own right. So it was just about encouraging each other and sticking to the process, sticking to the standards we were setting ourselves.

That was really the conversation, there was no massive roaring or shouting. It was just execute the plan, execute the plays, and then get those finishes.

We had been making chances, we just weren't taking them.

We could sense things were turning our way, we could feel it. We could feel it from the crowd. It was just relentless. We were winning kickouts… I got a couple in-a-row, and we won a couple of breaks. We could sense the tide just completely turning… we were getting more and more confidence.

That ultimately led us to the win.

If you were giving a mark out of 10, more of our lads would have gotten a higher mark in the second-half compared to what they might have gotten for the first. We imposed our game on them, we imposed our physical strength on them… we imposed our speed, pace, execution of the skills, and that's what led to the result.

If you were looking for the perfect game you'd say ideally it'd be great if we did it in the first-half too. That was the lesson we learned there; it has to be a full game, a full 70 minutes if we're going to win a Connacht title.

You'd be measuring yourself too.

I'd the cruciate ligament done two years prior to that so, for me, I was delighted to be in a Connacht final again but I could sense there was something in the group.

You could just feel that there was energy within it; there was an ambition there and you knew lads were all on the same wavelength.

But we still only took the Connacht final as another game.

We didn't want to get caught up in the euphoria. There was talk about what we were going to do, because we had the choice of venue, whether it was going to be Castlebar or the Hyde.

As Tommy always said, 'This is a dress rehearsal for the Connacht final.'

99

MARK BREHENY

(NOEL McGUIRE
& MICHAEL McNAMARA)

SLIGO 1-10 GALWAY 0-12
Connacht SFC Final
Dr Hyde Park
JULY 8 2007

Beating Galway to win the Connacht title in 2007, with his brother as manager, is the greatest memory of Mark Breheny's career with Sligo.

★ **SLIGO:** P Greene; C Harrison, **N McGuire**, R Donovan; P McGovern, **M McNamara (0-1)**, J Davey (0-1); E O'Hara (1-0), K Quinn (0-1); B Curran, B Egan, S Davey; D Kelly, **M Breheny (0-4)**, J McPartland (0-2). Subs: K Sweeney (0-1) for Egan, P Doohan for O'Hara, A Marren for Kelly, B Phillips for McNamara.

★ **GALWAY:** P Doherty; K Fitzgerald, F Hanley, D Burke; M Comer, D Blake, D Meehan; J Bergin, N Coleman; J Fallon (0-2), M Meehan (0-1), N Joyce (0-2); D Savage (0-1), P Joyce (0-5), C Bane (0-1). Subs: B Cullinane for Meehan, N Coyne for Blake, M Clancy for Coleman, P Geraghty for Savage.

THE ACTION

THIRTY-TWO YEARS of agony and pain came pouring out at Roscommon's Dr Hyde Park as Sligo banished the demons of previous years to clinch a third-ever Connacht title.

Though the final scoreline indicated a one-point win, there is little doubt that Sligo should have won this game by a more comfortable margin. Indeed, the number of missed opportunities the Yeats County racked up could – and almost did – come back to haunt them.

History, however, weighs heavily and Sligo knew they were on the brink of a famous success. After an enterprising opening with Kieran Quinn and Mark Breheny on target, Galway soon hit their stride and established a 0-5 to 0-2 lead midway through the first-half.

Then came one of the iconic moves in Sligo's footballing history.

A precise foot-pass from Michael McNamara was met by David Kelly, who collected and dished off possession to the on-rushing Eamonn O'Hara.

Still some 45 metres from goal, the Tourlestrane man showed a clean pair of heels to Joe Bergin and rifled a cracking left footed shot to the roof of the net to give Sligo a major boost.

It was a lead that Sligo clung onto for the rest of the match, though as opportunities went by the wayside to establish a more comfortable lead, memories of previous defeats began to flood back. This Sligo team, however, were not to be denied.

Centre-back McNamara kicked the insurance score to put Sligo two up, 1-10 to 0-11, in injury time, but Galway almost snatched a draw.

They kicked a 13-metre free to reduce the gap to the minimum, before Ja Fallon's attempt with the final kick of the game sailed towards the posts. Time stood still, but mercifully, it went narrowly wide.

★★★★★

66

I GOT THE call to come into the squad first in September 2000. Peter Ford had taken over after Mickey Moran stepped down and TJ Kilgallon came in with him. I came in and was really excited. I had watched those lads play in the years previously to that and wanted to be part of it.

The training was tough, I have to say… in Tubbercurry's back pitch for the most of it. We travelled to Enniscrone sometimes… temporary lights used to be put up in a field near the leisure centre. There's a hill there and we had to run up that with medicine balls – Jarlath Cunningham from Crossmolina was innovative and he brought a lot of different ideas to training.

Even at under-21 with Mickey Moran, we used to go out to Mullaghmore. There's a strip of grass there, so the lads don't know how good they have it in a pitch out in Scarden now!

That's where things were at the time.

We'd get a bag of fruit off Reggie McNulty afterwards on a Tuesday or Thursday night… there might be a mini Mars bar, with an apple or an orange and a banana. We'd hit the road then and that was it.

They were in the Connacht final in 1997 and that for me was the big eye-opener – and for a lot of Sligo fans. We hadn't seen anything like that before – the last final before that was in the early-80s. I couldn't believe the crowd that day when Sligo played Mayo… the black and white flags. I always refer to the fact that you couldn't even buy a jersey in Sligo town at the time.

I made my debut in 2000 against Meath in the National League and then in the championship we got the draw to play Kildare in Croke Park. The qualifiers really opened up Sligo to a national level again and people got more exposed to Sligo football. There was the TV coverage and everything that goes with it, the changing of the white to the black jersey… it just rolled from there and it was brilliant to be a part of. As a young lad you're saying you want to be part of this for as long as you can and experience the glory days.

In 2004, James Kearins came in and in fairness to James, he probably instilled a huge amount of confidence in myself. He gave me the No 11 jersey and told me, 'You start dictating things from here… start getting on the ball and leading from the front as a forward.' For me, that was probably the bit of an arm around the shoulder that I needed at the time just to move myself on in my career.

Again, playing Division One football that year we were a point off in scoring difference from getting to the league semi-final. We had won the FBD... we beat Mayo in Castlebar and the crowd on the pitch after was amazing.

Eamonn O'Hara lifted a cup that day and to actually get a bit of silverware was important.

In 2006 Tommy came in, in a caretaker capacity after we were told Dom Corrigan wasn't going to be involved anymore.

From there then, it actually started to kick off.

There's one moment that sticks out.

Myself and Tommy were travelling together back from Louth, where we had just been hammered. We were in the car... looking at our own attire. We had no proper gear at the time and we were both thinking... *We have to get this sorted.* Fellas were coming to games with different tops. It was just a small, subtle change that could help bring us in another direction again.

Louth had been well kitted-out. I will always remember them getting off the bus in their O'Neills gear and matching bags.

We also really started to look at our stats.

Tommy was big into that at the time, looking at videos – that's something we didn't do much of before. Gym work started with Trevor Coen, so we knew something was happening again. We felt momentum was good and Tommy got the backing of the players. He had played with the likes of Eamonn and Paul and the older lads, and he would have coached a few of us with St Mary's. Plus he was involved as an under-21 selector in the early noughties. He was in a good position.

It never really affected me, I have to say, having my brother as manager, and it probably helped me to keep my standards high because I never wanted him to feel that he would need to have a conversation with his selectors about having to drop me for something. Maybe that kept me on my toes more than being complacent.

At the start of 2007, Tommy said, 'This is it lads!'

That was putting a marker down straight away for everybody, in saying... *Right, it's now or never... if we're going to do it, let's do it now!*

We'd been through it; we'd come close as minors and under-21s in making the breakthrough. At senior level, we lost to Galway in 2002, and there were the Croke Park narrow misses, so we all felt… *Right, this has to be it… nobody is getting younger here.*

The squad was as strong as we'd probably ever had it.

In a county like Sligo, you might get a guy going travelling one year. Or work commitments might take a lad out of the squad, and all of a sudden we could be a little bit depleted – we didn't have the strength in-depth to compete with the other counties in Connacht.

Tommy did have that self-belief, and he did send out that message quite firmly saying… *This is it… let's knuckle down and train hard and see where it brings us.*

It just started… we gained momentum and training was really good, and Kieran Quinn and Michael McNamara were also on board.

We were going okay in the league, until we got beaten by Wexford which was probably a bit of a turning point in the year. A few harsh words had to be said about the way we were playing at times against Wexford – everybody had a frank conversation in the dressing-room. Nobody was really giving out, but everybody wanted to give things a certain direction and maybe look at a few little tweaks; there was nothing major.

Tommy took it all on board, and he added his own thoughts… it was great, it was just an informal chat really but everyone knew then we were back on track.

We'd probably look back at two games then in the league – one was against Antrim in Markievicz Park. I think we were five points down with 10 minutes to go in the game and the way the leagues were then, if you finished bottom of the group you'd go back down to Division Four. They were looking to restructure the leagues again.

That win was huge; we beat them by a point or two. And that then brought us to Wicklow, where we had to win down in Aughrim.

It was a big game. Mick O'Dwyer was manager of Wicklow but we'd a really good performance that day. It was a Bank Holiday weekend and we ended up having a few drinks that night and again maybe on the Monday, and the mood was brilliant. We knew in six or seven weeks' time we were going to be heading to New York.

The Wicklow game gave us a big confidence booster heading into the New York game. We knew it would be a tough challenge but Tommy had us fairly well psyched up.

New York brought Roscommon to the brink the year before so there was no complacency in the squad, we didn't want to be the first team to lose over in New York. We hit the ground running straight away over there.

The Roscommon game was a really important win.

The crowd were coming on to the field – it was the first time we had beaten Roscommon in Dr Hyde Park since the 70s. And we were trying to make our way to the dressing-room as quickly as we could.

It wasn't that we didn't want to be talking to fans, but we felt we'd been there before, getting the slaps on the back but having no cup to be shown at the end of the summer. We decided we'd all go in.

There was a realization that yes, it was a huge win, but this can't end here and we need to push this on and win this final when we get there.

There was a weight of expectation and a lot of mental scars from being so narrowly defeated in so many finals – going right back to the minor final in 1996 when Sligo were a point up and four minutes of injury time gone. Mayo chipped a ball out to Stephen Rochford.

He clipped the ball over the bar from out the wing.

I was only 15, listening in on the radio that day and couldn't believe it. The replay came back to Markievicz and we lost by a point. I lost myself to Leitrim in the 1998 decider.

Other lads had won big games at under-21, but lost in finals.

We lost in 2002 to Galway… so a lot of us had been through the mill and were thinking… *Will we ever get over the line?*

But I have to say, on the day itself, it's a feeling I'll always remember… I was so relaxed because of all those defeats.

I'd been through it all… if another defeat happens, it *happens.*

I got over it before… I'll get over it again!

So for me, I left all inhibitions behind me that day and just thought… *Let's go for this and whatever happens… happens.*

That was a general feeling.

Though the team meeting the night before was quite emotional.

Tommy had a video made up. There was nearly a tear in fellas eyes watching it. It was clips of our games that year, and the music with it was a song that we were fond of over in New York… and it all came together in that video. I think when lads left that room that night, there was a particular belief.

You know what, something special is going to happen tomorrow.

Even coming in to the ground that day, Tommy had a TV at the top of the bus; his preparation was meticulous. It was going to take us three or four minutes from Hannon's to get there. We'd a Garda escort, but that's as long as the DVD was going to last. As we were getting off the bus, the DVD was coming to an end… and we were into the dressing-room. The heads got onto it then.

We got a great score early on from Kieran Quinn out the wing.

Galway were chipping away and were attacking us down the wings especially. Nicky Joyce had a very good start to the game, Michael Meehan was going okay… Jarlath Fallon was probably their main forward and he was their most experienced player really. But they also had Derek Savage and Michael Meehan, and Pádraic Joyce was still playing. They were strong all over. They'd won the under-21 All-Ireland the year before as well, and had a couple of great players coming through.

The early free was important for me, it settled me… and then the second one came. Then I got a point on the loop. David Kelly was only new into the panel really at that stage but we knew each other so well and I could always rely on him to pop a little ball to me – he was very smart that way. I won a few breaks and set up a bit of stuff, I was feeling good.

Maybe at that stage I was getting a bit more experienced, but I knew how a centre-back was going to mark me. Diarmuid Blake was marking me, and he was sticky... very, very tight. It was very much a man-marking job.

He wasn't really interested in holding the middle, so once I was taking him out of that central area, it started creating more opportunities for other players. I read that fairly quickly in the game and tried to get on as much ball as I could.

All of a sudden then, the move came.

The O'Hara goal.

And that just erupted the stadium really, and brought more lads into the game. John McPartland got two great scores and led us in at half-time in a really great position.

But Galway were always going to come back at us and throw stuff at us.

Actually, looking back, they were very quiet in the second-half and that was probably down to our defence, though we let them off the leash with a couple of frees we missed. The pressure was beginning to build because if you miss one, the pressure is even greater on the next one. But our defence was holding tight still.

We knew we were creating opportunities. I think in other years, if we had missed certain opportunities, we might have folded, but not in that particular game.

We knew we needed to get that insurance point at the end.

Charlie came up the field. Kenny Sweeney had the ball in the corner, and it was knocked out of his hands and into mine. I caught it and sent it out to Michael and he kicked that score, and it was huge.

They had one chance.

We just couldn't wait for that whistle. Ja Fallon had that last chance, and the crowd behind the goal I can remember so clearly; the Hill Boys on tour, there was a huge crowd from that side of Sligo town and it was amazing to see the lads there, but once we saw them cheering I knew it was wide.

The ball left his foot – outside of the left… he is fairly proficient at that – and it sailed narrowly wide.

Immediately after, you're transported from the pitch to the podium.

Noel McGuire made a very passionate speech and my distinct memory is looking around and seeing ex-players. Brian Walsh and other characters who were on the squad when I came in and they had just missed out. I always felt for those lads… David Durkin, the likes of Paul Durcan.

Dessie Sloyan had retired the year before so there were a lot of brilliant players who had narrowly missed out. Going back to the 80s and 90s, John Kent, Fintan Feeney from Easkey, really talented players that would've graced any Sligo team over the years; they missed out, and I remember seeing those men after and saying, 'You know… this is for ye as well!'

You see family then straight away.

I still have photos… my dad was over the moon, my mum was delighted… brothers and sisters, and with both myself and Tommy involved it was a very unique and special thing for our family. I'm not too sure if there has been a combination of two brothers – one manager and one playing – in a Connacht final.

For me, growing up in the town there was a strong influence of soccer.

I remembered the 1994 celebrations with the FAI Cup and the crowds outside the Town Hall. It was our turn leading into the town and the bus arrived then in front of the Belfry; the road was just packed with people from every part of Sligo.

I carried the cup off the bus with a few of the other town boys and it was really, really special. That brought us into the Belfry then and the celebrations began properly.

I've been lucky there have been a few standout games over the years – 2002 against Tyrone, and my first game in Croke Park, and then in 2015 playing with my nephew Cian and being captain when we beat Roscommon… a little bit of revenge for 2010.

But when you do look back, 2007 is the big one.

NOEL McGUIRE

Noel McGuire had the honour of lifting the Nestor Cup in 2007.

66

I CAME INTO the panel about three weeks before the Connacht final in 1997. Sligo had beaten Roscommon in the semi-final. I'd finished the Leaving Cert that week, and I remember going to Markievicz Park on the Sunday.

I don't know where I bumped into Joe Queenan, who was involved in the backroom team at the time.

'You might be getting a shout!' he said to me.

We actually played Enniscrone in the Senior Championship around that time, in late-June of 1997 and a week or so later I was asked onto the panel – I was a sub for the Connacht final which was really exciting for an 18-year-old.

I was involved with the minors in 1996, agonisingly losing the Connacht final to Mayo following a replay after being 10 points up at half-time in the drawn game. I played under-21 for the following three years. While we got revenge on Mayo in 1999 for the minor defeat three years earlier, we lost the final to Roscommon. We were expected to win that final and we went up to Hyde Park full of hope, but it didn't go our way at all. It was a very difficult defeat to take for me as I was team captain and felt more responsibility for the loss.

Things were definitely on the upward curve though at that stage.

Mickey Moran was the manager and he had a very good reputation as a coach with Derry and subsequently went on to have further county and club successes. That time, we played National League football in the autumn, maybe six or eight weeks after the Connacht final, when we met Dublin and Kerry.

I started college in Dublin in September 1997.

I remember coming home on the bus on a Friday afternoon and the person beside me had a copy of the *Irish Independent*. In those days the teams for the weekend would be printed in the paper the previous Friday. I asked the man beside me if I could take a look at the paper... and found the Sligo team to face Dublin. To my delight and surprise, I was listed at corner-back to face the Dubs. That's how I found out I was making my debut. Needless to say, there have been big changes since then!

We'd a great run then... we beat Kerry in Tralee, beat Dublin... we had some great league performances and there was massive interest in the competition. We'd big crowds in Markievicz for the home games and there was a real buzz around the team and the progress we were making.

In terms of the physical training, I didn't find it that big of an adjustment. Mickey Moran's training was based on skills, drills and game situations. At that time many teams were getting slogged at training and running miles around mucky pitches.

This wasn't Mickey's approach, thankfully!

I actually found Sigerson Cup training to be more severe than the county training; there was a few tough weeks with the college in the winter time. But Mickey was everything about ball in the hand.

Sigerson football was a great experience and really prepared me well for county competition. We (UCD) were in the Sigerson final in 2000 but lost. It was a three-day weekend. We beat GMIT on the Friday after extra-time, we beat NUIG (our hosts) on the Saturday and we lost to Queens after extra-time on the Sunday.

It was another very difficult defeat to take. In the space of nine months I had lost a Connacht under-21 final, the county Senior Championship final with my club Easkey, and now the Sigerson Cup final.

We got to the final again in 2001. We beat Sligo IT along the way and I had to deal with marking my club and county team mate Dessie Sloyan in that game. We had a pint or two afterwards, so no falling out! We lost the final again, however, as an experienced, bearded and long haired Jimmy McGuinness inspired Jordanstown to victory.

Later on that year, thankfully we got our act together and we won the Dublin Senior Championship, beating St Vincent's in the final. Some silverware at last.

I remember actually, Dessie got married that Autumn.

We were playing Kilmacud Crokes in the Dublin quarter-final and I was at his wedding the day before. I was playing wing back and was doing okay. I wasn't setting the world on fire or anything but Ray Cosgrove was in his prime and was causing a bit of bother at full-forward and I was moved back on him. That's when the overload of the Guinness started to come out but, thankfully, we got through. Different times!

While it was an honour, I also found it difficult at times to be involved with so many teams. When I was a Fresher, I was asked onto the Sigerson panel to train and there was a situation where there was a clash… an under-21 Hastings Cup game with Sligo and a college league match. I decided to go home for the under-21 match. I was captain!

On the following Monday evening I was walking into the dressing-room for Sigerson training but I was ordered to get out… told that I'd chosen my allegiances and my services were no longer required.

While it was a lesson learned, if anything it was a relief as I was probably trying to do too much. I had no regrets about it. I cannot see a situation like that arising nowadays where player welfare, loading levels and rest are so important.

Sligo were very competitive in those years. We were probably a bit unfortunate not to win a Connacht title in those years around the millennium.

Galway were very strong at the time; they'd been in a few All Irelands, and it was difficult to beat the likes of them at that stage. But we were competing with them. We just couldn't get over the line to win the finals we were in at that stage. The introduction of the qualifiers and the backdoor gave us that lease of life that even though we hadn't got the provincial success, we had something else to aim for – and the way the draws fell for us, in 2001 and '02, we were in Croke Park!

In a way, it probably took a little bit of pressure off us in that we were able to just have a little bit of a cut, but we were also able to show what we were capable of doing and we did that pretty well.

We were so close in 2002.

We felt maybe we were finally at the top table… playing in an All-Ireland quarter-final, playing in Croke Park on a regular basis and it was a great experience. But it would have been nice to even get to a semi-final, it would have been a massive thing for Sligo at that time but, unfortunately, we didn't make it. You have to take those opportunities because the next year or two we struggled to get to that level.

There had been a good few changes between 2002 to '07; some lads had moved on and there were new, younger lads on the squad. We had a couple of average years in between but Tommy Breheny came on board halfway through the league in 2006. We'd a poor start but we finished that year quite strong and lost a qualifier to Westmeath that we should have won. We conceded a goal with the last kick of the game.

In 2007 we had a decent enough start to the league; we were in mid-table. But we had to go to Wicklow; Mick O'Dwyer was over them and they had been on quite a good run. We had to go to Aughrim to get a result and ensure we didn't end up in a relegation battle.

It was played on Easter Sunday – we stayed in Dublin on the Saturday night before the game. We were really well prepared for the game and knew what had to be done. We absolutely blew Wicklow away, leading by 10 or 12 points at one stage. They got a couple of scores at the end.

I had a really good feeling after that performance of what we were capable of and really started to think that something could happen that year.

We'd a trip to New York then only a few weeks later… first round of the championship. And that was a great experience because we had the group together for a week, as we stayed on for a few days after the game on the Sunday. We had a bit of craic but we trained hard as well and that brought the group really close together. I didn't really expect to be captain at that time.

I had been made captain just previous to Tommy coming on board. At that stage, they had kind of rotated it between some of the older and more experienced lads in the squad and I happened to be the last one that was captain.

Tommy came to me and said, 'I know you were captain for the last match and I don't see any reason why we should change that if you are happy enough to continue'.

I just said I'd be delighted to and that's how it happened.

We got over New York, and then we knew we had to go to Roscommon in the semi-final but really felt that we were in with a shout that year and that's the way it turned out. We had an average enough first-half against Roscommon. One of their goals was from Karol Mannion. I was marking him, and it came from a turnover; we were just making some silly mistakes in that first-half.

We were five or six points down at one stage but we didn't panic. I do remember that in the lead up to the game that while we were very focused, we were a bit edgy as our record in the Hyde wasn't great.

We didn't get out of the blocks in the first-half like we should have done.

But we kept the heads and saw it through; we scored maybe eight or 10 points from play in the second-half. Paul McGovern had a blinder, Brian Curran got a couple of great scores… it was just one of those halves where we clicked. It was a great feeling winning that game and the way we went about it. Previous years we wouldn't have responded to the situation that we were in. It was a good feeling coming home.

The run in to the Connacht final is a little bit of a blur in my mind. I don't have any stand out memories of the few weeks leading into it. I don't know what the reason for that is.

I do remember John Murphy, the chairman of the County Board, ringing me on the Saturday on the eve of the final and asking me had I my speech prepared and telling me not to forget to mention certain things.

'Grand!' I told him. 'I do have a few words in the back of my head… hopefully I'll need them!'

Another thing I remember is when I was leaving home that morning. I said something to my mother about lifting the cup and what it would be like. She has often said to me since, 'I felt so sorry for you when you were leaving that morning!' She obviously didn't think we'd a prayer!

But obviously a 'winning' mindset was with me then.

It's easy to say now, but that feeling that I had after the Wicklow game was obviously still imbedded in me.

On the morning of the final, we met at Clifford Electrical in Carraroe; they were our sponsors, and Philip Greene was a couple of minutes late. He got a bit of slagging (those who were brave enough to slag him). As a group we were confident, had kept the heads down and we were definitely in the right frame of mind.

I've watched bits of the game since and we probably should have won by five or six points but we only scraped it by a point. We'd a bad day on frees, a lot of missed chances. Ja Fallon had a shot at the end, off the outside of the left, but it went narrowly wide.

There was one other incident in that game just before Ja Fallon's late effort. Barry Cullinane came through and I hit him a shoulder but it was right on the edge of the small square.

It was a split-second decision whether to make the hit or try and hold him out, but he was a powerful man coming at pace.

He got a free (I thought it was a fair hit!) and they tapped it over but I often look back and think... *Jesus, it was a risk to take, an inch or two more closer to goal and it's a penalty!* But I just about got away with.

I was marking Pádraic Joyce for most of the game.

At training, management would put you marking a left footed player so you could get used to certain movements. I would have marked Joyce a few times up to that and would have had difficulties with him because he was one of the best footballers in the country and remained so for some time after that.

That day, he and Michael Meehan were switching quite regularly so while I had my work cut out for me, I was well prepared.

You just try and concentrate on your own game as best you can.

We would have looked at clips of them individually and as a group and what they like to do on the ball. *Would they take you on? Would they like to play it to someone else and take it back?* Things like that.

I think it's fair to say we dominated the game for long periods.

We probably had most of the possession but we weren't that economical with it. Obviously, the goal is a standout point in the match because it was executed so well. A long kick-pass from Michael McNamara to David Kelly, and he lays it off to Eamonn on the run and at that stage there were two or three lads trailing in his wake.

He soloed with his right and hit it with his left... an unbelievable goal.

And that was the difference. We got one really clear-cut goal chance and we took it even though we did miss a good lot of chances on the day. We would have done that before and ended up drawing a game and losing a replay, but we just managed to do enough on the day.

Towards the end I was thinking... *If we could get one more!*

We were just hanging in there, but we didn't panic. The Ja Fallon effort – he ended up shooting on the left hand side off his left foot. We didn't let him cut inside, make a pass and narrow the angle.

We didn't panic, whereas other days we might have given away a free. We kept the heads when it was required, and it worked out.

It was mayhem at the final whistle.

I turned around and Philip Greene was closest to me... bear hug!

Charlie was up the other end of the pitch and I think Ross had Derek Savage hounded out to the corner flag at that stage.

Next thing we were just completely engulfed by the supporters.

It was absolute carnage. After a few seconds it was nearly impossible to find any of your teammates... people jumping on your back and all that.

Then lifting you up... it was just crazy.

I've never experienced anything like it before or since. It was a unique and special situation to be in. Getting over to the presentation area, I don't know how long it took, but we got there eventually.

In relation to receiving the Nestor Cup, you think about these things and you're saying to yourself ... *You'd never know...* but until that actual moment, you don't actually realise the meaning of it and what's happening.

It's a bit of a haze really.

I do remember the presentation area wasn't very stable. They had an old table, maybe four foot by three foot, and to stand up on that with your boots on… it was wobbling all over the place. Trying to keep myself standing on it was the main thing. I think John McPartland managed to stumble off it!

We had a couple of great nights with plenty of craic. On the Monday, we went out to Strandhill for a while and then we got a bus out to west Sligo. We came into Dromore West and turned right heading for my village of Easkey.

I had been hearing there'd be bonfires and this and that, and I was saying back, 'Will you don't be daft!'

But as we started getting closer, it wasn't only Easkey people that were out, it was all of west Sligo…bonfires and all. Those couple of hours that evening, all the players in the village, going into the pubs, were very special.

I remember meeting my mother and father and brothers that evening, and they were so proud of me carrying the Nestor Cup into the village. My father JP was particularly emotional – I had never seen him like that before. It was the standout moment for me.

It was great meeting friends, relations, neighbours, people I had known all my life… lads I had played with, chatting with them and having the craic.

Kevin Walsh was over us for a few years after. He had won a couple of All-Irelands, Connacht medals, All Stars, but he often used to say that he remembers the ones he lost more than the ones that he won.

There would definitely be regret that we didn't back it up and win another Connacht final, especially in 2010, after beating Galway and Mayo that year. We probably took our eye off the ball a little bit and lost to Roscommon. I feel we had such calibre of players that we should have won one more Connacht title and to have had the chance to play in an All-Ireland semi-final would have been great.

Overall, I was involved from 1997 until 2012. I maybe stayed on a year or two too long but it really consumed me. It takes over your life really!

Other things are put on hold. There were a lot of highs, probably even more lows but there are a lot of players that have gone before and played since and don't have a Connacht medal to show for it. I am forever grateful for that.

99

MICHAEL McNAMARA

Turning his back on Sligo Rovers' demand to be a full-time professional set Michael McNamara on the road to Connacht Championship glory with Sligo in 2007.

"

THERE IS A difference now compared to then.

I remember when I first came into the senior squad in 2001, being up in Enniscrone at the back of Waterpoint; a field with a generator and that was the year I was coming back from doing the cruciate so I was a bit tentative, but we were going up the hill, mud up to your ankles, and I was thinking… *What am I doing here?* With Sligo Rovers, the training was very, very different. Sometimes with Rovers, we'd do a 12-minute run and the lads would be giving out!

You see lads training in Scarden now and there's no comparison with the facilities. That time, generally we'd be up in Tubbercurry on the back pitch and again the muck was up to our knees but that was all part of it, and it built character too.

At that stage, I hadn't made any decision as to what I was doing. I was between both soccer and gaelic football and really you could do that because the seasons allowed it to an extent back then.

In 2002, I came on against Leitrim in Markievicz Park. Sligo won easily, but I came on at the end for two minutes and I just remember being a bag of nerves. It was a miserable auld day; we won easily but I was still nervous coming on.

I didn't play much that year, until the Armagh replay.

I came on in Navan. I got 15 or 20 minutes and that was a baptism of fire because it literally was a red-hot battle. It was a roasting day, very heavy, and things were very, very tight. I remember quite clearly giving away a free for a score, and then getting a free to make a score. So that was the start of it.

I went back to Rovers… was back and forth a bit and in 2004 under James Kearins I played, it was probably my first proper year.

We were beaten by Clare in the qualifiers. I was playing corner-forward, there was no ball coming in and I got a bit disillusioned by the whole thing to be honest because you're doing that level of training and football back then, it was very different then as it is now… positions meant something back then and you were supposed to stick fairly rigidly to where you were playing.

I was stuck in the full-forward line and thinking… *Am I sure about this?*

I got the chance to go back to Sligo Rovers, once we were knocked out of the championship, and I kind of stuck there until 2007 really.

At the start of 2005, Sean Connor had come in as manager of Sligo Rovers and I was nearly at a stage where I needed to make a decision.

He made me captain that year; we'd a great year and got promoted from the First Division. It was really enjoyable. There was a good mixture there and in 2006 we were in the Premier Division – it was the first year I didn't go between the two sports, I stayed the full year with Rovers.

At the end of 2006, I had fully intended on staying with Rovers. But a lad called Rob McDonald came in, and he basically wanted a full-time set-up. There were a few of us that were part-time and everyone else was full-time, and he more or less said to us it's go full-time or nothing.

I didn't really want to do that. I was working full-time as well and didn't want to take that chance. So that was an abrupt end to the Rovers.

I had a couple of options in terms of other clubs but, to be honest, I wasn't that interested to go off and play elsewhere, it just wasn't my thing. I was very happy with Rovers but was not going somewhere for a few bob just for the sake of doing it. And as it happened, Tommy Breheny got in touch and that was that.

It probably would have been towards the end of 2006 when Tommy spoke to me.

I had a conversation with Kieran Quinn too, asking him if he was going back in? And that was important, not that it was a decision-breaker for me but it was a big part of it because you could see there were a few lads coming back. I had played a lot with Kieran too, I'd a lot of time for him.

Things added up right and, apart from that, just meeting Tommy, he was just so positive about the whole thing; he said this is my plan... this is my plan for you and that was it really. I liked his positivity and there were lads back, so it looked good. I didn't need too long to think about it.

My first impressions were that I was way off the pace, because I was coming in from Rovers and soccer, and I was kind of shadowing defenders and stuff like that. I remember Tommy saying, 'You need to get closer here!' I was just way off.

But from the start, there was a good bond, a good crew and good craic from the early days. The training itself, it was very tough but it was organised and ball-orientated. I would say Tommy was ahead of his time to a certain extent; you were doing an awful lot of running but you were doing it without realising it because a lot of it was with the ball. It was enjoyable, which made things a bit easier.

I think New York was a very big factor.

It was a good result, but it wasn't just the result itself.

It was always good to put up a decent score against New York because, as we've seen, they can be a bit of a bogey team, but we put them to bed fairly early. But there was training after, craic after and everything that went with it, that really brought the group together. Still to this day there's stories we'd still have the craic about.

They are stories I wouldn't tell, but still!

I was getting there at centre-back. It did take a little while, but I was getting a little bit more confident as the year went on. Positional sense, trying to add more value to the team and all that.

Come the Roscommon game, we'd a poor first-half and for teams in the past that could have been enough to see us off. Then we go in for the half-time chat, come out and concede a goal straight away again.

But there was some character. I would always see Brian Curran as an unsung hero of that team; he got through some great work in that game and the Galway game. Paul McGovern, another lad, he was fairly quiet but super-efficient. Quinner, no more than myself, was growing into things as well.

For me, there was a side aspect to it, as both my parents are from Roscommon and all my extended family live there. My Granny was alive at the time and she was living there. So that was an added dimension for me, because I would have grown up going to an awful lot of games in Roscommon. I remember warming up on the second pitch in the Hyde, and my dad was there and he came over to shake my hand and you could nearly see the emotion in his face, so it all came together nicely to be a big game for us.

I think it gave us a bit of belief because we were no longer talking about doing this and that – now we were actually doing it. We had come back and came back well in the game. Tommy's attention to detail was serious, he had us coming into the final very well versed. All the little things added up to a lot and we did go into the Connacht final thinking we could win it.

The build-up was good; you're always going to be a bit apprehensive, you're playing a fancied team with fellas you were watching growing up… the Ja Fallons and Pádraic Joyces!

We did an early part of a warm-up in a school a couple of miles away which was a good idea in hindsight because you're away from all the hype of it on the pitch but you're getting a sweat up, you're getting focused.

I remember quite distinctly, we were really on it. We were doing things right, there was no real messing going on. It was just focused on actually getting warmed up and every kick or anything was being done right.

I picked up Michael Meehan mainly that day… he came out to centre-forward.

Ja Fallon was there for a while, and Pádraic Joyce as well as they rotated a fair bit but in the main it was Meehan. I wasn't the tightest of man-markers. I always liked to get on the ball and try to set up plays. What you're trying to do is you're trying to get tight to these lads, and they are serious players.

There were a couple of incidents in that game, early on, where if they had taken their chances they would have had a couple of goals. We probably rode our luck a little bit in the early stages, but for me I was just trying to get on as much ball as possible, especially in the early part to settle myself.

I remember my last ball before the goal. I put it straight out over the sideline with a bad kick so I was really anxious to get on another ball quickly.

Although it wasn't a plan as such, we used to always work on in training hitting the lads in the inside line and their big thing – and what Tommy always said – was to bag the ball. Whatever sort of ball went in, he wanted to make sure they were hanging onto it and taking it, and then decide what you'll do after.

David was a great fella to play with; he was always on the move and he was so quick; he'd make a bad ball into a good ball a lot of the time. I loved playing with David.

O'Hara just took off, and in hindsight and talking to Eamonn, he says when I got it he took off; he probably got the yard on his man before I kicked it because he knew where it was going. It was an incredible goal. I have it as one of the best goals Sligo ever scored just in terms of importance and the sheer power and pace of him, and then to finish with his left foot.

We went in at half-time and we were dying to get back out on the field, thinking we hadn't enough done at all; there wasn't a puff out of anyone. That was the vibe, that we'd so much more to bring to it.

The second-half, we were conscious we were missing chances. I was definitely conscious of it. Derek Savage said to me late in the game, 'Ye should be out of here... this should be over!'

For whatever reason, they weren't going over.

I suppose the weight of history and everything else had an impact and took its toll. We should have been ahead by more but who is to say we would have won it? We could have gone ahead, taken our foot off the pedal and they'd come back and get on top. It was anxious at the time but it worked out alright.

The likes of Paul McGovern and Johnny Davey were great lads to have either side of me in the half-back line, and then behind us Charlie, Noel and Ross – at the time they were, to me, one of the best full-back lines around; they had to have been and they were.

It was a tight unit. Every ball, we were ravenous to get around it or get around a fella. If you went to someone there was always another man coming behind you, and that wasn't a planned thing, it just sort of happened. It happens with good players.

It was a nice six to be involved in, a good defence.

It's funny when people talk about the point I scored at the end because after, I remember Philip Greene asking me what the hell I was doing up there anyway?

Whatever way It worked out, and it'll be nice in years to come looking back on it, myself and Charlie, two John's lads, worked our way up the pitch. It went into the corner a bit, but we retained the ball well.

I probably fouled the ball, just in the lead up to it. I sort of jumped over a tackle and the ball was on the ground, and I sort of tapped it along the ground and Charlie just stuck his foot out and managed to keep it.

Breheny then passed the ball to me, a low pass to me around my shin area.

I was slagging him after saying it was an awful pass, but he said he couldn't give it any higher because there was a defender there. In hindsight, he was right, and it probably worked out better because had it come to me in a normal position I probably would have thought about it a bit more.

But I didn't think at all.

I knew where I was and I just swung at it and I was more surprised than anybody to see it go over the bar to be honest! It was just an instinctive thing. If I had time to think about it, it mightn't have happened.

I went off. After the move with the point my back spasmed totally and I didn't want to be standing there, struggling and be at fault for anything so I said to the lads to get me off and get someone fresh on to do a job. Brendan Phillips came on, and it was excruciating the last couple of minutes looking on, to see Ja Fallon miss that last chance… I'm sure he put them over in his sleep before.

It was unbelievable when the whistle went.

I was sitting against an ice box at the time, literally just sat there.

I think one of the physios came over to give me a hug and then I went on the pitch. Some of the slaps on the back, it was hard to breath at times! But getting out there to see the lads, it was a great feeling and something that will live with us forever.

I remember getting off the bus in town. Barnes Murphy was there and a whole load of underage coaches from over the years and it was emotional; it was a huge thing for us. I didn't expect anybody to be there. We went through the more rural spots and we saw the bonfires and people out, but I didn't expect it in Carraroe. It was a nice surprise… lovely.

Things have changed an awful lot now.

Back then, you went out and you celebrated a good win, and maybe you went out after a loss too. But that's what you played for, and that's the stuff you'll remember in years and years to come… the craic. There are loads and loads of stories of the day after… two days after… three days after, being up in Gurteen, Easkey, all sorts of spots, signing young fellas foreheads and jerseys. Just carnage really, but in a great way.

I might have missed it all if the manager didn't change at Rovers.

I was happy where I was, captain of Rovers and no reason to leave. You look back and think, there were a couple of lads who had retired before 2007 and I know they would have been looking at it and were delighted, but deep down I'm sure there was a bit of regret with them too.

If I wasn't involved, I would've been over the moon for the lads but you'd always have that thought… *Could have I been involved… could I have gotten that opportunity?*'

DAVID KELLY

GALWAY 1-10 SLIGO 1-10
Connacht SFC Semi-Final
Pearse Stadium
JUNE 27 2010

David Kelly shows Galway's Alan Burke a clean pair of heels in Pearse Stadium in 2010.

★ **GALWAY:** A Faherty; K Fitzgerald, F Hanley, A Burke; G Bradshaw, D Blake, G O'Donnell; J Bergin (0-1), P Conroy; G Sice (0-1), S Armstrong, N Coleman; E Concannon (1-1), P Joyce (0-7), M Clancy. Subs: M Meehan for Clancy, D Cummins for Conroy.

★ **SLIGO:** P Greene; C Harrison, N McGuire, R Donovan; K Cawley (0-1), B Phillips, J Davey; T Taylor (0-1), S Gilmartin; C McGee (0-3), M Breheny (0-1), A Costello (0-1); K Sweeney, E O'Hara, **D Kelly (1-3)**. Subs: E Mullen for Sweeney, S Coen for McGee.

THE ACTION

AS FAR AS near misses go, this draw at Pearse Stadium was among the most gut-wrenching for Sligo as they watched a nine-point lead evaporate and saw Galway earn another bite at the cherry.

Gareth Bradshaw's late free saved the hosts blushes after Sligo dominated the vast majority of this encounter.

On a typically blustery day close to the Atlantic, Kevin Walsh's visitors came into the game on the back of an impressive opening win over Mayo and continued in a similar vein of form in the opening 35 minutes.

With David Kelly and Mark Breheny to the fore in the first-half, Sligo totally controlled matters and went into the dressing-rooms at 1-8 to 0-2 in front at the break. Kelly's 30th minute goal – which featured a lung-bursting run from a wide position before a deft finish – was the icing on the cake of a first-half performance which also included scores from Colm McGee and Tony Taylor.

Galway looked stunned, and even in the early stages of the second-half their fightback amounted to little. Sligo would only register two second-half scores, though when Man of the Match Kelly fired over in the 70th minute, the visitors lead remained five points, 1-10 to 0-8.

Galway, to their credit, never gave up the fight. The key score came in a lengthy period of injury time, when they blasted home their only goal.

Pádraic Joyce initially cut the deficit to four with his sixth point, before the veteran forward was centrally involved in laying off a pass to Eoin Concannon, who rattled the Sligo net.

There was still time, too, for an equaliser. Sligo protested when Michael Meehan won the Tribesmen a kickable free 25 metres out. The claims were in vain, as Gareth Bradshaw popped over the equaliser and sent both teams to a replay in Markievicz Park.

★★★★★

"

THERE WAS A confidence in the group ahead of the championship in 2010.

That period in training was probably the most enjoyable I've ever had. I think I was probably playing some of the best football I was ever playing at the time and training was just so enjoyable.

Mayo was always the big game. I don't know when we had last beaten them and they were going through a period of transition. But they had John O'Mahony in charge and they'd some brilliant footballers, unbelievable forwards.

But we did take confidence from the previous year, and from the league especially and getting promotion. Having Mayo at home, in Markievicz… a gorgeous day… big crowd. We were confident going into it but not thinking we were going to walk away with it. And after them giving us that trimming two years before, that was one of the worst and such a kick in the teeth! But we were a different team in 2010.

That period started in 2009 when Kevin Walsh came in as manager.

We won Division Four, and there was a real sense of togetherness – winning breeds that as well. Galway beat us in the championship, but the game against Kerry showed we could play football with the best, that we'd some brilliant players. It does give you the belief that you can get up to these higher powers, these super teams, and it definitely helped us going into 2010.

I remember going in at half-time during that Kerry game and I couldn't get my breath. I didn't know what it was, but I was nearly feeling like I was going to collapse! But I remember the tunnel and going in at half-time, and I've never seen fans like that. They were going ballistic, absolutely ballistic.

I didn't pay huge attention to it, but I remember there was just absolute fury on the way in. The second-half took its own path. I know people will remember the penalty but I'd a couple of '45s' too that went narrowly wide as well.

A penalty miss definitely affects you. Of course, football gets in your head and puts you in bad form, but I always try to park it – and my wife Edith has no interest in football. I'd say she has been to two of my games in her entire life, and we could have won the All-Ireland or lost in a relegation play-off and it'd be the same response.

I get away from football.

I love it, but I do get away from it. The penalty, it hurt at the time, more so because you feel like you're letting down your teammates a little bit but they make you realise fairly quickly that you're being daft and these things happen. Someone has to do it; it didn't work out, it was a bad penalty.

There was a delay before taking it, and it definitely did affect me. The cute Kerry trait; they delayed it for so long that when I went to take the penalty, I remember feeling my legs.

Looking back now, people use it sometimes to slag.

Stephen Gilmartin, who is a bit of joker, for my stag party he got onto Diarmuid Murphy to get the jersey he wore in the match so I'd have to wear it for the weekend of the stag!

I was first called into the panel in October of 2005.

It was one of the best days of my life. I couldn't believe it; I was still in school in Leaving Cert.

I got this letter, real official, and it was such a big thing and it should be a *big thing* because it's such an honour to represent your county.

I still have the letter.

I felt like a child. I was 18.

By 2010 I had built myself up a bit. I'd featured in Sigerson Cups in 2008 and '09 with DCU. In 2010 we won the Sigerson, the first since 2006. I played really well, and I remember winning Player of the Year too.

I probably didn't really think about it initially, but also I was saying to the Sligo lads, 'I'm playing for DCU with some of the best players in Ireland, and I'm an influential player on the team. And I see Sligo, and there's 10 guys here that I think are brilliant and better players'.

I fed off it, got huge confidence off that but I think other players did too. I remember saying it to guys; I remember having a conversation with Charlie and saying there isn't a huge difference.

I didn't see a massive difference between us and these big teams, I really didn't.

At that time, it might have been delusional, but I felt we could win Connacht titles, definitely, and go further. You're in a bubble when you're an inter-county player, and you are a little bit deluded and you need to be, but there was unbelievable belief that time and DCU definitely gave it to me, playing with guys who were making me better.

We'd come off the win over Mayo. That was a huge win and gave us even more belief. I wasn't ever big on records, saying Sligo hasn't won here or whatever... I wouldn't have a clue. Those types of stats never came into my head.

We were thinking we're in the best possible shape we could be in, we're after beating Mayo who are one of the big two and we're heading to Galway.

I always liked playing against Galway, at underage or senior.

And having Kevin in charge of us definitely gave us another bit of confidence, that we had this Galway legend who knew Galway inside out, and he was going to prep us in the best way possible. I remember his team talks in Markievicz Park, going through the Mayo team, going through the Galway team, and he knew everything about them.

We were playing some really good football too, and probably should have been scoring a little bit more even.

I remember one specific training session out in Tourlestrane around that time.

I used to always try and mark Ross. Ross was one of our standout players, he wasn't just one of the best corner-backs in Sligo but in the country over so many years; he was unbelievable. Charlie too, and he would test you differently.

Ross and myself used to have big battles.

But at that time, I didn't care who came on to mark me, I just had that uber-confidence that they can't control me. Marky B, Alan Cos, Stevie G, Tony Taylor... lads were playing ball in who were just brilliant passers of the ball.

I felt if I was getting good ball, it didn't matter who was marking me.

I was loving training.

We'd a wind in the first-half in Salthill.

It was down the pitch, and in the second-half I'm not sure if it calmed a little but it was still windy and we'd too many wides and balls going into the keeper's hands. There were a few fellas Kevin mentioned that could be marking me, but all he used to say to me that time was, 'Go at them, take them on... keep going at them!' They were probably trying to isolate me in there a little bit.

Before the goal, I'd a point and it was probably half a goal chance and I remember thinking at the time I probably should've taken him on and gone for goal.

Marky B and Alan Cos, those two were class. I always loved playing with lefties, even in college with Ronan Flanagan or Shane Roche. In Mark and Alan, they were two completely different passers of the ball, but you couldn't find two better.

I was getting on ball. I never thought of myself as a big scorer, I always considered myself more of a playmaker.

Even with the club I always loved playing at No 11.

I got on ball, laid off a few, so I definitely started well and the confidence was flying by the time the goal chance came around.

It was the terrace side, but in towards the middle.

The ball came across, and I ran out towards midfield and I was out around the '45' when I got the ball. I got it out in front and you're always feeling out a marker – how they are doing it, are they from the front, are they tight, are they jumping a little.

When the ball was coming to me, I saw my man making a bit of dart for the ball and I remember getting the ball then and just stepping him. That gave me the yard and all I could see is green grass, and I just took off.

And then I could just feel that he wasn't gaining on me – sometimes you're going towards the goal and you can see someone coming towards you, so you veer to the side and just pop it over. But I could sense that this lad wasn't going to catch me.

I was able to just go straight for goal.

The lads had got out of the way. We'd great movement at that time and all I could see was the goal. It was probably a bit daft – and people probably would have been giving out to me after if I had missed it – but I took it on my right and my man was on my inside. I felt I had enough space to use the right… just saw the far corner and pinged into the far right side.

I just placed it in there, it wasn't blasted.

Kevin used to give out to me a lot, because my usual first option was to pass.

It was like… 'Score, score… SCORE!'

It took me a while to get that mentality, and Paul Taylor used to do a lot of work with me that time on that, about being selfish, about going at them. So, when you get through like that, and you see the space, you go for it.

You don't have a huge amount of time to think about it so you hope the decision you make is the right one. Whoever was doing the camera flew in on Mark Breheny coming out, after me scoring the goal.

Mark used to slag me about that... him getting credit for it!

When we came in after the first-half, we were full of confidence.

But that second-half was really poor from us... yes, we were into the wind, but we took on bad choices.

I was angry that there wasn't enough ball coming in. But we took on some poor shots, and I remember thinking to myself... *If I get the ball there is not a hope in hell I am going to pass... I'm going at them!*

We dropped balls short... kicked wides. They kicked 1-2 in the last four minutes and it was a real big kick in the teeth after being such a good performance for 50 minutes; we dropped off in the last 15.

After the game, I was like a bull... we all were.

It was like the same thing... *Typical Sligo, do well for a while and then draw the game!*

I was taken in for an interview with RTÉ, and I was furious.

The management team were walking by, and I remember Paul Durcan, who was a coach at the time... really good, he was brilliant. He came in and just signalled to me to keep the head up, focus on next week. And it was just a flip of the switch in my head; I still remember it to this day.

He was saying it was time to stop feeling sorry for myself.

It's onto next week.

I don't know what I would have said in the interview, but I went from rage to... 'Brilliant, yeah... we get to play them at home next week!'

It was the same in the dressing-room.

We get the opportunity now to beat them at home. And that game at home were different conditions, but that was an unbelievable win.

Collie kicked a brilliant score towards the end. In those games I was playing with Colm and Stephen, who were two of my best friends my whole life, and the buzz was unbelievable.

I was 72 or 73 kilos, I was a feather and I used to tape the jerseys, because fellas would be pulling the living daylights out of me. I used to like a tight fit under the jersey, and I wore this white Under Armour and it just became a thing. I was working at summer camps and young bucks would be coming in wearing this white Under Armours.

When I was living in Crossmolina when I was very young, I used to be babysit by a certain family, the Costellos, and one of their daughters Bernie, lives in Castleconnor now.

I was coaching their children over at the camp in Enniscrone and I remember signing their white Under Armour tops! It was mad.

But it happened.

I'm not a superstitious person at all. I would have habits, but I wasn't a 'lucky sock' person. But I did have a few of those white Under Armours, and I did wash them!

99

ROSS DONOVAN

SLIGO 1-14 GALWAY 0-16
Connacht SFC Semi-Final Replay
Markievicz Park
JULY 3 2010

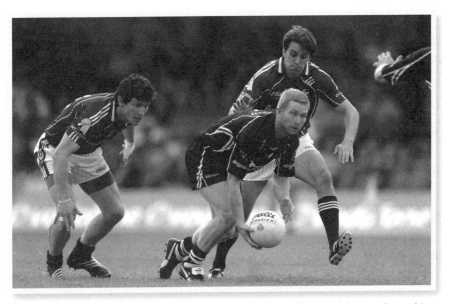

Ross Donovan kept some of his greatest performances in the Sligo jersey for meetings with Galway.

★ **SLIGO:** P Greene; C Harrison, N McGuire, **R Donovan**; K Cawley (0-1), B Phillips, J Davey; E Mullen, S Gilmartin; E O'Hara, M Breheny (0-4), A Costello (0-1); S Coen, A Marren (0-3), D Kelly (1-2). Subs: C McGee (0-2) for Coen, S Davey for Costello, K Sweeney (0-1) for O'Hara, F Quinn for Marren.

★ **TEAM:** A Faherty; A Burke, F Hanley, K Fitzgerald; G Bradshaw, D Blake, G O'Donnell (0-1); J Bergin (0-1), N Coleman; G Sice, S Armstrong (0-4), M Clancy (0-2); M Meehan (0-1), P Joyce (0-5), E Concannon (0-1). Subs: P Conroy (0-1) for Meehan, D Reilly for Hanley.

THE ACTION

A RAUCOUS ATMOSPHERE, a gutsy Sligo performance and a stunning finish meant a wet July night in Markievicz Park went into the annals of the county's GAA history.

Having suffered the deflation six days previously of snatching a draw from the jaws of victory, Kevin Walsh's charges finished the job – but only just – to book their place in a novel Connacht final against Roscommon, the first Connacht decider without Mayo or Galway since 1947.

The visitors opening half display suggested Sligo's poor replay record looked destined to continue. At 0-8 to 0-4 in front as half-time approached, the Tribesmen were motoring well with attacking talents such as Pádraic Joyce, Michael Meehan and Seanie Armstrong all finding range. Prior to the interval, points from Mark Breheny and David Kelly helped trim the deficit at the break to two, 0-8 to 0-6.

Momentum firmly switched in Sligo's favour shortly after the resumption, when Gareth Bradshaw's loose sideline ball back to goalkeeper Adrian Faherty was intercepted by the ever-alert Kelly, who slotted home to inject real belief into his side's prospects.

Galway, to their credit, reeled off the next three scores in retaliation, and found themselves two in front as the game entered injury time. This is when Sligo made their decisive move. Timing their runs to perfection, Kenneth Sweeney and Mark Breheny – off his right – brought Sligo back level as the home support grew in anticipation.

Amid near unbearable tension, Colm McGee, sprung off the bench and having already kicked a point, connected sweetly with a left-footed effort from range to send Sligo folk everywhere into delirium, even if Galway protested that the ball went wide.

★ ★ ★ ★ ★

"

WHEN THE FINAL whistle went, I was still coming down from the sensation of the winning score and the reaction from the supporters, that was the best feeling I'll ever take from county football. Pádraic Joyce turned and said all the best and I replied thanks… and I walked to the sideline. The crowd was going mad.

It is amazing how time can change or alter a memory of such occasions.

When I was asked to talk about a game in my playing career that stood out for me, I jotted down a few notes from memory and what I could remember from the game as it unfolded.

Then, as it happened, I found an old recording of the game and watched it back. It was amazing how much I had forgotten.

At a young age, playing at under-16 and minor level, I never had a grá for county football. I remember a club man of mine ringing once or twice to come into a panel, but I had started working at the age of 17 in a job and the hassle of going into Sligo for training just didn't appeal to me. I wasn't a big Sligo GAA man.

It wasn't until under-21s that I eventual joined a panel; another Harps man was involved, Dennis Johnson. It was there that I enjoyed the training sessions and the buzz of competing against the so-called best in the county. Unfortunately, I broke my hand a few weeks out from the championship game and didn't feature on the day.

But I had got a taste for county football and really enjoyed it.

However, it wasn't until 2005 that I first got the shout for the senior squad. I was turning 23 that summer.

Dom Corrigan had been appointed and he's the only man I can remember who held full out trials. I still remember those sessions; we were run at the start, put through our paces for what felt like forever and then we were put into a full match.

In 2009, Kevin Walsh was a massive boost to Sligo football. He brought an aura around the place when he landed. And he was such a big man you couldn't but look up to him, especially with what he had achieved in the game.

Obviously he was one of the best managers I trained under; he did great things with Sligo football. He brought us so far. Look to where we got with him.

He knew where he wanted to take us and maybe with a bit more luck or the bounce of the ball we should have won a Connacht title under him.

We did win two National League divisional titles, and earned promotion to Division Two.

I always think of that year in Division Two in 2011. Donegal got away with a draw by the skin of their teeth against us in Ballybofey; we gave away a silly penalty – I can still see it today- and then we were beating Laois comfortably up to half-time in Markievicz Park and we didn't come out for the second-half.

They were two results that would have kept us up. It's funny, Donegal and Jim McGuinness went one way that year and we went the other.

But we had a great group of lads under Kevin, all very driven and they'd drag you with them if they had to. We all trained very hard and very few men stepped out of a training session or anything like that.

I think what came off the back of those league wins in 2009 and '10 was, you went the extra yard. We were ran, and we were knocking lumps out of each other – you would barely be able to walk coming off the training field. You'd just about make it to the dressing-rooms but once you made it to the shower and finished up, you couldn't wait for Thursday night.

We would have done weekends too – training Friday, Saturday and Sunday. It wouldn't be all training on the field; we would have meetings and other preparations to get through.

We used to do great bonding sessions with each other. Kevin was great for taking us away the odd time and doing something different. One year we went to Donegal, and we were running through lakes and running up mountains, crazy stuff. Some lads were afraid of their lives that they wouldn't be ready for championship in a few weeks.

Men couldn't believe this is what we were doing before championship. But it all stood to us and I felt great after some of those experiences with the lads.

But Kevin was great for preparing us coming up to games and one feature of that included opposition stats or notes – player profiles if you like. I was never one for information on who I was marking, I never usually minded, but some men gobbled up that stuff.

The information would be on A4 sheets and would be passed around the bus going to a game or the night before after a meeting. What I liked about it was, it was passed around. It was a case of take it if you want, or leave it if you want.

I always tell the story… one evening on a bus and we were playing a league game. It was the first time these sheets had taken off, and I gave them the full works.

It read… 'Never takes his man on directly and is right footed'.

So I read that and sure enough this man comes into my corner.

Maybe five minutes into the game, a diagonal ball came across the pitch, 30 yards from goal out on the sideline. I just completely closed off the right side, to invite him onto his left.

Jesus, he put the head down, took me on and smacked it over the bar with his left foot! I spent the next five minutes trying to figure out if I was on the right man. I was looking around thinking… *I have the wrong man…* and wondering what his information was.

I concluded at that moment that that was the end of those sheets for me!

After that, I just looked at the sheets the odd time.

Either way, good county players are two-footed for the last 20 years. Dublin didn't bring in the two-footed player. I've marked some super footballers from Wexford to Antrim that could kick off their left and right.

Kevin did have certain ways he would like us to play but I mostly played my own way, what I was comfortable with. I hated playing out in front of certain lads because they were so smart behind me.

Andy Moran was a man I'd never mark out in front.

I still laugh at lads trying to mark him three yards in front. Andy's so sharp, when you'd look at him he'd move right and when you react he's gone the other way. I go off their shoulders… the likes of Andy.

Other lads that might be slow… I'd play out in front of them all day because even if I get it wrong, I'll be able to make it up.

I always played the man.

I was fortunate to experience some great days in the county jersey, but the reason why the Galway replay in 2010 sticks in my mind is the atmosphere and the crowd.

If you asked me the score I wouldn't remember... I know we won by a point. I thought the weather on the day was fine but I've been informed it was raining.

But the reason that game sticks out in my mind is the atmosphere. I've played in Croke Park. But every time I played there, I could hear the seagulls and birds chirping around, so I never really took to it.

I'd have loved to play there with a full house, but that's what the Galway game in Markievicz Park brought. We had a full house. And Markievicz is nice when it's full; the terrace comes right around and the noise from the stand comes bellowing at you when the supporters roar.

What I remember are the last few minutes and the roar when we equalised.

The hairs on my neck and arms started moving, but you're still in the game and you're focused. I was on Pádraic Joyce at the end and all I was thinking was that I needed to keep him quiet.

When we got the equaliser, I remember feeling that little tingle, but then we got the winner and I swear to God, I've never had a feeling like that in any other game... just the crowd's reaction... the roar.

It's what I expect a full house in Croke Park is like.

It is something I still talk about and the fact that it was in Markievicz! Our home crowd, and without a doubt that was what sealed it. Galway didn't know where they were when the roar came out.

There was no way we were ever going to give up a score after that... the roar!

I was marking Joyce, and I just thought to myself... *I'm delighted to be marking him because he is the man the ball will come to... if it comes up!*

I was buzzing.

Watching the game back you can see the excitement in the county as the pitch was invaded and you would swear we had won a major trophy.

I couldn't finish without a mention of the Connacht final we played on the back of beating Galway that year. Unfortunately we lost that game.

People will say that was a final that got away and that Sligo should have won, but they don't give you a reason why it did or why we should have won. Just because you beat Mayo and Galway.

We had no entitlement to win that game.

It was Sligo vs Roscommon, neither of us were ever winning much. I watched that game back only in the last lockdown, May 2020... it was a ding-dong game.

But I do think we could have played much better; we were much better that year than we showed on the day. We had opportunities either to draw level or go ahead and I was looking back thinking… *If just one of them had gone over the bar, it could have been different.*

But you can't take anything away from Donie Shine of Roscommon, he couldn't kick a blade of grass wrong that day.

I still get annoyed when people say we should have won that game. You're not entitled to anything.

But I do believe we should have played better.

I am one of the few fortunate Sligo players to hold a Connacht medal, from 2007. That was a fantastic achievement for Sligo and I did enjoy the success, but maybe at the time I was younger and easy going; it was more a sense of just taking it all in.

I wasn't used to winning or losing Connacht finals at that stage.

All in all, I am very grateful for my time with Sligo GAA, and it isn't for all we achieved or won. It is for all the great friends and times we had along the way, and for that very special day in July, in Markievicz Park.

99

ADRIAN MARREN

GALWAY 0-15 SLIGO 2-14
Connacht SFC Semi-Final
Pearse Stadium
JUNE 9 2012

The belief of manager Kevin Walsh was so important as Adrian Marren went on a personal mission to demolish Galway in the 2012 championship.

★ **SLIGO:** P Greene; N Ewing, J Martyn, R Donovan; C Harrison, M Quinn, P McGovern; S McManus (0-1), E Mullen; A Costello (0-3), P Hughes (0-1), B Egan; M Breheny (0-1), **A Marren (2-6)**, D Kelly (0-2). Subs: T Taylor for Mullen, D Maye for Hughes, J Davey for McGovern.

★ **TEAM:** A Faherty; K Kelly, F Hanley, K McGrath; G Bradshaw, J Duane, G O'Donnell; J Bergin, G Higgins; G Sice (0-3), D Burke, T Flynn; S Armstrong (0-1), P Conroy (0-3), M Hehir (0-7). Subs: M Meehan (0-1) for Flynn, G Sweeney for Kelly, P Joyce for Burke, C Forde for Hanley.

THE ACTION

THEY SAY RECORDS are there to be broken – and Sligo shattered one of the longest-standing in the province on a sunny June day in Salthill.

The county's dismal record against the Tribesman on their home patch was summed up by the fact that they had not recorded a championship win over Galway there since 1922 – and on that occasion, the result was overturned via an objection, with Galway winning the replay in Croke Park by two points, and in the process denying Sligo the chance to contest their first-ever All-Ireland final.

History, however, counted for little on a pleasant evening by the sea when Sligo, under the tutelage of Galway legend Kevin Walsh took to the field with a bit of unfinished business.

Two years previously, at the same venue, Sligo put themselves in a winning position before allowing Galway back into the game, and ultimately snatching a draw. This time around, when the Yeats County got a sight of the finishing line, they powered for home to qualify for the Connacht decider.

Having overcome New York before the Galway clash, a tentative start saw the visitors trail by 0-9 to 0-5 at the break, but with the breeze at their backs in the second period, Sligo sensed a shock was on.

They emerged with real gusto after the interval, producing some superb football to stun the hosts. New recruit Shane McManus enjoyed a powerful afternoon at midfield, Alan Costello's left boot could do little wrong and the defence, backboned by Charlie Harrison and Ross Donovan, showed their mettle on several occasions.

Adrian Marren was to be the matchwinner, with a remarkable total of 2-6 helping Sligo to a five-point win, and a place in the Connacht final, their third in six seasons.

★ ★ ★ ★ ★

"

THAT DAY, KEVIN Walsh said to me in the dressing-room beforehand, 'I know we have all the boys back!'

But he continued talking, trying to instil a bit of belief I suppose, saying, 'You're our main man, you keep doing what you're doing… you've been our main man since I've come in. Just stick to what you're doing… I guarantee you it'll pay off today.'

And just the way the game panned out, it did.

I had come in during January of 2004, when James Kearins was manager.

I played a year minor when John McPartland was manager and I played under-21 when Denis Johnson was manager, though I only played under-21 in my last year. I hadn't got game time up until that.

I didn't commit to the senior squad before Christmas because I wasn't sure if I was going to go in or not; I was working in Dublin at the time. Then James Kearins managed to persuade me to come in. I came in then in late-January, because I didn't play in the first couple of league games.

I made my debut down in Wexford Park, around February or March. I would've been 21.

Football wasn't as serious for me until I was 16 or 17 – up to that I was just happy enough to be playing it and enjoying it. It was only probably when I got into county minor, that's when I decided that I liked it. I enjoyed playing it and took it a bit more seriously.

There was a very strong panel. Nigel Clancy was still there, Neil Carew was there, Pádraic Doohan was playing away… Paul Durcan, Eamonn O'Hara was in his prime then, David Durkin was still involved… it was a very strong team.

Those first couple of years I was probably just happy to be in there, having the craic. That time, after every league game it was a party. You'd go to the games with your going out clothes with you, that was the way it was.

We were happy enough to be in there, then, probably in 2007 after winning it, we knew then how professional it had gone. We played Cork in Croke Park after winning the Connacht final and we saw the way they walked into Croke Park – they were kitted out like they were going to a wedding.

It was a completely different level; they had a very strong team and won the All-Ireland three years later. We kind of knew what it was going to take and when Kevin took over in 2009 it really took off.

He came in and we never trained anything like it.

We were super fit, the training was awful hard. Kevin brought in these one kilometre runs that we had never done with Sligo before. The start of a training session was four 1ks, and you wouldn't be fit to walk after it.

Then you'd have to go in and do a full session after that.

But in the long run, it stood to us. We flew through 2009 and '10 and even 2011 in the league up in Division Two, we were very unlucky to be relegated. We probably fell flat in the championship that year; the relegation probably had an effect on us.

We used to train a lot in the back pitch in Curry and the back pitch in Tubbercurry. We used to play this game… 'Murder Ball' was the name of it, where you couldn't use your foot to pick the ball up, you couldn't kick-pass… any of the rules you were supposed to be playing by you couldn't play by those rules.

And on the back pitch in Curry or Tubbercurry, you're up to your ankles in mud. It's probably something no player had come across or done before… everything went. And you just had to suck it up because there was no complaining, you were just told to get on with it.

The Kerry game in the qualifiers in 2009 stands out.

We flew down. Everything was new that time. We went to Knock Airport, to get the flight down, but we got held up in traffic… the game got held up by 15 or 20 minutes. I don't think people were expecting the crowd that was down there.

It was absolutely wild.

We went in at half-time two points up. David Kelly was after getting a goal and that time going in in Tralee you went in through a tunnel, and there was a cage over it and they were pegging bottles of Coke at the Kerry players… the Kerry supporters!

They were gone mental.

They were expected to go and give us an awful trimming but definitely we should have won it. We had plenty of chances. Just their bit of extra experience and class told in the end. Paul Galvin had a massive game that day.

It would have been one of the biggest shocks.

There was a bit of a changing of the guard in 2012. A few of the older lads had stepped away and a few of the younger lads had come in… Pat Hughes, Shane McManus, Stephen Coen… all of those lads had come in and were starting.

We hadn't a great league campaign; we didn't get promoted or anything but we won a few, lost a few, and we didn't get relegated either. Championship was a great shot for us because we went over and played New York, which helped us a lot as in getting a win over there and a bit of team bonding.

Then the Galway game! There was great confidence because it was set up for us.

A semi-final against Galway in Salthill meant we were big underdogs, but Kevin had everything done on Galway. We knew everything about them, he had them off to a tee.

It just worked out absolutely perfect on the evening.

Even in FBD, we would have beaten them handy in some of those games. We weren't afraid of Galway, and we weren't afraid of Mayo either in those years. That was the kind of confidence that we had because we had a lot of wins under the belt.

We beat Mayo in 2010. The Connacht final in 2012 was close… that was James Horan starting with Mayo and probably that was another Connacht final we should have won.

I felt good going into that Galway game.

I was after having a good league and it was great to be playing in the forwards when you had David Kelly beside you. He was probably our marquee forward and he used to take that little bit of extra attention.

If they were dropping a sweeper back, David was always going to get that extra little bit of attention so you always knew you were going to get chances when he was in there with you because he would take that extra man – or if he made a run, he'd draw that man so he would free up space for me and a bit of time. It was great.

They'd a bit of a breeze in the first-half; they were 0-9 to 0-5 up at half-time and they looked comfortable, they were in control.

We were chipping away really – they were getting scores a bit easier.

But we'd a good chat at half-time, and Kevin told us to just go for it, that the spaces will open up… and the second-half just went well for us. We actually ended up winning quite handy, by four or five points in the end. Probably 15 minutes into the second-half the game was over.

We were trying to not lose the game in the first-half; we were dropping boys back and that. But we still contained them and hit them at the break and kept chipping away at the scoreboard. Just trying not to be too much down, not to concede a goal and not to be too far behind at half time.

Kevin had told me that Finian Hanley was going to be picking me up, and I had been marked by Finian quite a bit between the FBD and championship. I knew one-on-one with Finian he was going to beat me in a race.

But Kevin told me keep going sideways… keep moving… 'You'll create space for yourself', and I just kept doing that and I created a lot of space for myself and got on more ball than I ever did.

David used to be inside.

Pat Hughes used to come in and out.

Alan Costello was a great advantage for us. We knew inside if we made a run, it was definitely going to land in our arms or land close enough that we could run on to it – he was a great man to pick a pass and play a pass. It was a great advantage for us inside, and when he left the following year, he was a massive loss for us.

I think I kicked three in the first-half; I think I had three shots and the three of them went over. The breeze kind of died in the second-half… it was a bit dull in the first-half and then it brightened up into a lovely evening in the second in Salthill.

Finian Hanley took a knock off Paul McGovern for the penalty, and he wasn't right after that and I can't remember the lad they brought on but it was open country then. It just worked out… it was just a game where it worked out.

Always when I'm taking frees, I take my five bounces so I have the same routine. It's the same for penalties, I always face the O'Neill's right towards me, so that's what I'm keeping my eye on.

I know where I'm going anyway. I take one look at the goal and that's it.

I'm just concentrating on the ball and getting the right connection and once you get a sweet connection… you know it's going in.

We got a great bounce off the penalty and I think we went two or three points up at that stage… and we just kicked on. People were saying it wasn't a great Galway team, but they brought on Pádraic Joyce and Michael Meehan as a double substitution after that penalty. I don't know, were they holding them back thinking they'd get over us and have them ready for a Connacht final? I know Joyce was coming towards the end of his career at that time but still it wasn't a bad Galway team.

The second goal came when we turned them over.

The ball came to Alan Cos, and I used to always make this run where I'd look to move forward, then check and go sideways.

And Cos knew my run and he put the ball into my lap and I caught the ball… and went BANG!

Adrian Faherty was in goals, and I would have known him. He was playing with IT Sligo at the time and we would have played them in a lot of challenges. I'd say he thought I was going to take the ball on.

But where I was, and that bit of confidence as well after kicking a few scores… I just went for it and… BANG! I think it was in the net before he realised what was after happening.

It was game over after that.

NIALL MURPHY

SLIGO 1-14 ROSCOMMON 0-13
Connacht SFC Semi-Final
Markievicz Park
JUNE 20 2015

Niall Murphy thought manager Niall Carew was 'nuts' when he first asked him to man a midfield berth on the Sligo team.

★ **SLIGO:** A Devaney; R Donovan, K McDonnell, D Maye; K Cawley, B Egan, E Flanagan; C Breheny (0-2), **N Murphy**; C Davey, M Breheny (0-2), N Ewing; D Kelly (0-1), P Hughes (0-2), A Marren (1-7). Subs: B Curran for Davey, S Gilmartin for Breheny, J Hynes for Cawley.

★ **ROSCOMMON:** D O'Malley; S McDermott, N Carty, N Collins; N Daly (0-1), D Ward, C Cafferky (0-2), I Kilbride, C Shine; R Stack, C Cregg (0-4), E Smith (0-2); D Murtagh (0-2), S Kilbride, C Murtagh. Subs: C Connelly for D Murtagh, D Smith (0-1) for Stack, D Keenan for Ward, C Compton for S Kilbride, F Cregg (0-1) for C Murtagh, M Finneran for Shine.

THE ACTION

A FIRST-HALF PENALTY from Adrian Marren sent Sligo on their way to a fully deserved four-point win over hot favourites Roscommon at Markievicz Park.

The visitors – who had claimed the Division Two league title a couple of months previously – came to town with huge expectations but they were firmly halted in their tracks by a Sligo side who qualified for a first Connacht final in three years.

On top for the vast majority of the 70 minutes, one of the key features of the winning performance was that of their forward unit, where Pat Hughes, David Kelly, Mark Breheny and Man of the Match Marren all excelled.

At midfield, too, Sligo's youthful partnership of Cian Breheny and Niall Murphy managed to keep the hosts ticking over.

Marren's penalty – after a foul on Neil Ewing – came shortly before half-time, with Sligo's interval advantage of five points (1-7 to 0-5) putting them firmly in the driving seat.

The home support was growing in confidence that a shock could be on, but Roscommon, even though not firing on all cylinders, managed to stay in touch with Enda Smith and Cathal Cregg among those driving the Rossies forward.

Sligo were always able to stay out in front, however, though they were fortunate to see Cian Connolly pass up a guilt-edged goal opportunity in the second period.

Mark Breheny fired over the final score to a rousing reception from the home support amongst the 9,500 attendance, as Sligo ended as deserved four-point winners.

★★★★★

66

I WON A Sigerson in 2015 and to be honest that year was a big wake up call for me in general.

We obviously beat Roscommon, and we got beaten by Mayo in the final, but I actually got dropped for the Sigerson Cup final so that was a huge blow. It was probably the first time I had ever been dropped.

Between being dropped there, and then playing against Mayo, a top side, I took a big look at myself and could see that I was way off the standard that I wanted to get to. Where I am now to where I was then, I was miles off.

I was probably four or five kilos overweight. I saw some clips of the 2015 game recently and I was at least five kilos over the weight that I am now. I wasn't fit, and college was probably getting to me, so that year probably gave me a big kick up the backside that I needed, to be honest.

In 2010, when Sligo beat Galway and Mayo, that had a big influence on me.

I remember going to those games; I think we might have played a minor game before one of them. My father was involved with St Mary's when I was at a young age; he was a selector in 2001 when they won the county championship; he was involved with Tommy Breheny. I actually grew up playing with St Mary's until I was 10 or 11. I would have lived in Kent Park a lot… I lived near there and that was my earliest introduction into football.

At that time, Mark Breheny would have been coming up… Johnny Martyn, Johnny Davey… I'd have been watching them at age seven, eight, nine, going to training to watch them… going to games to watch them, and seeing them out there.

I wouldn't have missed a training session.

We moved when I was 11 or 12. I didn't want to go at all. My mum is originally from Coolera and my Dad is a Donegal man. My parents ended up building out here and for the first year or two I remember I did not want to move to Coolera.

I remember the first training session, being brought to it and not wanting to get out of the car.

St Mary's won the championship in 2001 and I was nearly a mascot at that stage. Around that time too, I played games in the same year for Coolera and St Mary's – for one in the Community Games and the other in a club match.

It's amazing how time changes things. Now, St Mary's are probably our biggest rivals and I would give anything to win a championship with Coolera/Strandhill. I love playing with the club. It all worked out!

It was around 2012 that I got called in to the county senior squad for the first time. I didn't expect to get called in at that stage and I probably wasn't ready. I was a bit immature and my body wasn't right yet. I didn't have the mentality to play at that stage. I knew going in it was going to be hard work in terms of running and gym work and that, and it was *that* and a bit more too.

I was in college and there were times where I was training in the morning for DCU and then training that evening for Sligo; it was just mental. It would not happen now at all.

My appetite probably dropped for football, just the slogging and trying to juggle playing county football and college football as well. It was tough.

We lost to London in 2013 but it didn't have that big an impact on me... I was 19 at that stage. I came on that day, but in my younger years I had more of a carefree attitude, maybe I wasn't giving it as much as the other lads on the panel.

We didn't know a whole pile about Niall Carew when he came in as manager at the end of 2014. But in fairness when he came in, he set a high standard straight away. He put question marks over players and you knew from the get-go that he meant business.

When I look back on that year in 2015, we were so confident.

Halfway through the league that year, we really changed the system we were playing and what we were doing. Myself and Cian Breheny ended up playing midfield in the latter half of that year. We ended up winning our last three league games and then went on to beat Roscommon.

I remember going into that game thinking there is no way we're going to lose; you get that feeling for some games and that was one of them. Niall definitely instilled confidence in us and he had Ronan Sweeney there as well, who was an excellent coach, so I think over the first year or two he definitely brought up the standards big time.

In 2014 I played a lot of games but I got injured before the championship, so I didn't make the team and I actually went to the U.S. – the lads went on a bit of a run in '14 and beat Limerick and Wicklow, so I missed that.

I came in in 2015 and quickly he came to me about playing midfield.

I had never played midfield, even at club level. I was thinking this fella is nuts, *absolutely nuts!* I was nearly laughing. Johnny Doyle for Kildare got an All Star at midfield, and Niall said he played a part in moving him out to midfield – he was involved with Kildare as a selector with Kieran McGeeney.

I think his thoughts were that midfielders weren't really getting marked, they'd a lot of space, they had the most possessions of the ball and I think that's what he saw in the role for me. On the ball would be one of my strengths, so he thought let's get him into midfield where there's a lot of space, lots of time on the ball and ball touches.

That's the way he sold it to me and over time and over the next couple of years, I loved playing there.

Of course, when we played Mayo in 2015 I got a bit of a shock – the power and pace of those lads was just on a different level. There's definitely a lot more running and movement in that position, but you just have to be cute about it and know the times when to go forward or when to hang back a bit.

One or two games in, I was really enjoying it and I was going okay. We won three league games, beat Roscommon, the final didn't go well but Niall put huge confidence in me.

He was pushing me to play midfield, telling me to get on the ball… do this and do that… and he definitely put a lot of confidence in me. There were probably a lot of people wondering about Cian and myself as the midfield pairing but I think the few games that we did play there seemed to be okay.

For those games, both myself and Cian were very forward thinking, and probably not too defensive-minded. I think we did complement each other; Cian was very athletic whereas I was the ball player. He was able to get around the pitch a bit more and he was very good in the air.

At the time, the Sigerson didn't have much of an impact on my county stuff. I probably thought I should have been playing in that Sigerson final; I was going well with Sligo that year, playing all the time and felt I was playing well.

But when I look back on it, getting dropped for that game and losing to Mayo had a big effect when I was looking at where I wanted to get to.

After that year, I had a real look at myself and when I came back in 2016 I came back a lot stronger, leaner, fitter, quicker… everything. So those few things that happened over that time opened my eyes.

We had a lot of confidence heading into that Roscommon game.

They had won Division Two to go up to Division One, they were flying. We were going okay, I suppose; we had kept our position in Division Three but no one was giving us a prayer. But when I look back, I just never saw us losing that game.

I was living with a couple of the Roscommon lads in DCU at the time, the Smiths and others, and the lads would be giving us grief. And I remember saying – and you should never say this – but I was saying, 'I promise ye lads, we won't lose this game!'

It's amazing when I look back the way we were thinking. You might have a game like that once a year, or once every couple of years where you think we're not going to lose, and Niall definitely helped instil that in us.

I think we were all confident.

Niall liked to play attacking football and we had David Kelly, Pat Hughes, Adrian Marren and Mark Breheny all playing in a very high forward position, so I would think the lads, all of us, and the management, were confident.

From the start of that year, even in December and January, Niall was always mentioning Roscommon; it was always Roscommon. Now, you wouldn't look past the league but he always had Roscommon on his mind, and on the tip of his tongue during training.

We were building up to it from January.

Roscommon over the years have been down in Division Three and Four, but in 2010 Roscommon beat Sligo and I'm sure that was getting to some of the older lads. I wasn't involved for that but I'm sure for them, they felt like they had to get one up on them.

In 2015 I still had a little bit of a carefree attitude.

We started quite well. We were playing into the dressing-room end in the first-half and we got a penalty which Adrian Marren scored. We were up going into half-time and we were comfortable enough.

There was no real time in the game where I felt we were going to lose.